CHASING DOGS

MY ADVENTURES AS THE OFFICIAL PHOTOGRAPHER OF ALASKA'S IDITAROD®

TEXT AND PHOTOGRAPHY BY JEFF SCHULTZ

FOREWORD BY DEEDEE JONROWE

To order single or multiple copies of the trade paperback edition, go online to www.Iditarodphotos.com/chasingdogs

ISBN 978-0-615-94068-7

Iditarod®, The Last Great Race®, Iditarod Trail Sled Dog Race®, and Alaska's Iditarod® are registered trademarks of the Iditarod Trail Committee. Used with permission.

EDITOR: Tricia Brown
PHOTO EDITOR: Richard Murphy
DESIGNER: Elizabeth Watson, Watson Graphics
MAPMAKER: Penny Panlener
PRODUCTION MANAGER: Richard L. Owsiany, RLO Media Productions
PREPRESS: William Campbell, Mars PreMedia

Published by Jeff Schultz Photography, Inc., Anchorage, Alaska USA
www.schultzphoto.com
907-279-2797
info@schultzphoto.com

COVER: Jason Barron navigates the windswept ice of Farewell Lake, 2008. FRONT FLAP, TOP: "Dog boxes" on mushers' trucks constrain the dogs during travel. In Anchorage, Tim Osmar's dogs are keeping an eye on the action. BOTTOM: Dr. Terry Adkins' dogs, Fred Astaire and Roy Rogers, rest at Anvik, 1991.

TITLE PAGE: With a 20 mph wind at his back and a setting sun in his eyes, Charlie Boulding makes his way down the Yukon River between Ruby and Galena, some 50 miles downstream, 2000.

DEDICATION PAGE: Lachlan Clarke's father-and-son lead dogs, Starbuck (left) and Walter, trot in sync through a light snowfall outside the Finger Lake checkpoint, 2012.

TABLE OF CONTENTS: Warren Palfrey on the trail as the sun sets behind the Bering Sea, still several miles from the finish line in Nome, 2009.

PAGES 10-11: The 2014 race was marked by a lack of snow and an abundance of glare ice and wind. Here, Zeb Olson of Golovin watches as Norwegian musher Joar Leifseth Ulsom passes. Ulsom would finish in 4th place.

BACK COVER, CLOCKWISE FROM ABOVE, LEFT: Robert Sørlie, 2007 finish line; DeeDee Jonrowe in Rainy Pass; a frosty Kristy Berington, 2010.

ACKNOWLEDGMENTS

M Y FIRST ACKNOWLEDGMENT is for my friend and editor, Tricia Brown. We've worked on several books over many years. As usual, her experience, guidance, and the way she edited my words made this book really what it is. *Thank you, Trish!* And to the great team of people who also helped shape it on the front and back ends: Richard Murphy, Betty Watson, Dick Owsiany, and my assistant, Trent Grasse. *Thank you, all!* Recognition needs to go to my friends at the camera company, Canon USA, who have generously helped me with the best equipment through the years, especially Mike Gurley, and also to the fine folks at my local camera store, Stewart's Photo, especially Mike Ellis.

Many of my Iditarod photos simply would not have been possible if not for many friends and strangers who lent me a hand along the trail. First and foremost, a *huge* thank you goes to the late Joe Redington Sr. for inviting me to get involved with this great event back in 1980.

After thirty-plus years, there are so many others to list, and I apologize to any I may have left out. Thank you: Joy Berger, Greg Bill, Jasper Bond, Rich and Violet Burnham, Donald Covault, Danny and Susan Davidson, Joe and Norma Delia, Carl and Kirsten Dixon, Gary and Willa Eckenweiler, Chuck and Peggy Fagerstrom, Howard and Julie Farley, Dick and Audra Forsgren, Dan and Jean Gabryzak, Ron Halsey, Pat Hahn and Sue Greely, Stan Hooley, Maurice Ivanoff, Gary Jacobson, Doug Katchatag, Jake Kramer, Bill Luth, Sam Maxwell, Chris McDonell, Von Mitton, Steve Nelson, Jan and Dick Newton, Mark Nordman, Mike and Pat Owens, Carl Paul, Steve and Denise Perrins, Steve Perrins II, Emmitt and Edna Peters, Joanne Potts, Leo and Erna Rasmussen, Vi and Joe Redington Sr., John and Marty Runkle, Laura Samuelson, Doc and Frankie Sayer, Ben Schultz, Philip "Tucker" Semaken, Barry and Kirsten Stanley, Starre Szelag, and Buckey Winkley. Thanks to *all* who have helped me to "get the shot."

A bundled-up mob mills around the downtown Anchorage race start at 4th Avenue and D Streets, 2012.

Sharing the Trail

We were young, naïve, and full of adventurous spirits—mine with dogs and Jeff's with cameras, but same scenes.

I had run the Iditarod twice, fallen madly obsessed with the adrenaline rush and was determined to improve my competitiveness. In 1983, behind the lens of camera was a quiet, blond man with a beautiful smile. He rarely spoke, but was behind bushes, *clicking*, rock outcropping, *clicking*, standing on the village trapping trails into town, *clicking*. He became the sign that things would be okay no matter how cold it was or tired I was.

I still have on the wall a picture that Jeff took in 1991 when I was trying to encourage my team to wade into flowing water, 22 miles west of Kaltag on the portage headed over to Unalakleet. It was -25°F and the creek was open, flowing, and knee-deep. No time to discuss the wisdom of what we needed to do— just DO IT! I can remember like yesterday thinking, "Where did he come from?"

Since then Jeff has weathered the same storms, flown in conditions that nearly grabbed him to heaven much too early, and changed his life forever. Still, Jeff has continued to capture my life's dreams in pictures. He has become as iconic as the Burled Arch is to me when I close my eyes and think "Iditarod." I am bonded to Jeff's life's work at a level few people may understand.

—DeeDee Jonrowe
Willow, Alaska, 2013

Jeff Schultz, shooting in Rainy Pass.

DeeDee Jonrowe, attending to chores.

DeeDee encourages her team through that brief stretch of open water.

Lance Mackey runs in Ptarmigan Valley beyond the Rainy Pass checkpoint. Tripods often mark the trail in treeless areas and stay up year-round.

The Test of Time

The Iditarod tests a person in so many ways. And it's a rewarding test—I have learned this firsthand during more than thirty years as the official Iditarod photographer. Covering the event takes endurance, strategic thinking, tolerance for cold, patience, the ability to deal with mechanical, technical, or logistical problems, and make decisions on the fly. Oh, and it helps to have a strong back to pack a load of photography gear, among other necessities.

Through all those years, I've also seen that anyone who joins in making the Iditarod happen—in *any* way—is guaranteed the adventure of a lifetime, whether it's selling T-shirts in Anchorage, doing vet checks along the trail, shoveling dog poop at a checkpoint, or setting up tables for the finishers' banquet in Nome. Working the Iditarod, volunteers can claim a special badge of honor, something akin to celebrity status.

My job is volunteer work, too. The role was an opportunity that was simply handed to me in 1980 by the "Father of the Iditarod," Joe Redington, Sr. I had no qualifications, no interview, no portfolio review, or test. It was purely a blessing.

When I shot my first race in 1981, I had no idea what I was getting into or how the Iditarod would forever change my life. I was twenty-one years old and had been in Alaska for just two years. But this I did know: I was born for two things—adventure and photography. And for me, the Iditarod was, and still is, saturated with monumental opportunity for both.

That first year I was constantly out of my comfort zone. No two days were the same, no two hours were the same. *Where's the best place to be right now? Who*

Then: film and bunny boots, Rohn 1981.

Now: memory cards and duct tape, 2010. PHOTO BY STEVE PERRINS II.

do I talk to? Is that a working snowmachine? There were photo opportunities in every direction, things I'd never seen before. And I loved it.

Since the first running in 1973, the race has grown in popularity, and the state legislature voted to make dog-mushing Alaska's official state sport. The race is followed by people all over the country and the world. In Alaska, more people know who won last year's Iditarod than who won the Super Bowl.

Who wins doesn't matter to me. I don't have favorites, but I do smile when new blood enters the winner's circle. I simply enjoy chronicling what happens on the trail and I'm forever looking for the ultimate image—something that says "Iditarod" at first

glance, whether it's an Alaskan husky curled up on a bed of straw, a weary musher doing her dog chores, or a tiny team shot from the air, a mere dot on a vast, beautiful canvas.

After more than thirty years of chasing dogs and their mushers on the Iditarod Trail, it seems I've become a race fixture. I cherish my time on the trail, reconnecting with friends and watching mushers contend with the trail and nature. And that's what the Last Great Race does—ties people together and changes lives—for better and for worse.

Sometimes I think I've seen most everything, and yet the trail continues to throw surprises at me. Each year I can't wait to go back.

1

A Life-Changing Invitation

In 1979, I took my girlfriend (and now wife), Joan Wright, to a concert featuring "Dr. Schultz and the Last Frontier Band" (no relation), playing at the then-biggest arena in Anchorage, the West High School Auditorium. I was nineteen and had been living in Alaska for a year.

I didn't know the concert was a benefit for musher Colonel Norman Vaughan, and that the Dr. Schultz Band was the official band of "the Iditarod." *Whatever that was.* At intermission, someone took the stage and spoke poetically of a daring race, mushers who defied the elements, and sled dogs with the stamina to run more than a thousand miles. I was captivated. This was the adventure I'd been seeking when I left the pavement and people of California.

Several prominent mushers were introduced, including one of the race founders, Joe Redington Sr., whom they called the "Father of the Iditarod." He stood, just a row ahead of us. Joan leaned over and said, "Doesn't he have a kind face?" Her words ignited my thoughts. I had recently hung out my shingle as a wedding and portrait photographer. My big idea: "Create a fantastic portrait of a famous Alaskan like him, and I could become famous myself, or get lots of business." I could see the portrait already: Joe Redington in his sled-building log cabin, harnesses and sleds hanging in the background, wood shavings all around. Light streaming in from a paned window, bathing that "kind face" in a glow. A gigantic 30 by 40-inch sample of my work. Awestruck, people would engage me to do their portrait.

Just days after the concert, I wrote Joe asking if he would pose for me—some kid he didn't know from

Joe and I liked each other from the start. His enthusiasm for sled dogs in general, and the Iditarod in particular, was infectious.

Adam—and mailed the letter to his place in Knik, Alaska. Sometime later I received a reply: "I'm on the trail now. Write me in April when I'm back." *On the trail? What trail?*

By late spring 1980, I was driving my 1969 Chevy truck up a rutted driveway to the Redington place. I had expected a beautiful log-cabin homestead, complete with the log tack shop that would be his sled- and harness-making building with the sawdust on the ground. Reality set me straight.

I pulled in near three mobile homes—trailers, actually—amid huge piles of junk, a half-dozen

dilapidated cars, and a truck. Everything seemed to be overflowing with newspapers and other assorted trash. Stench wafted from a bucket of fish heads swarming with flies. *This can't be the place.*

Tentatively, I knocked on a trailer door. Out popped Joe's kind face, his ball cap askew on his head. "Wanna cup of tea?"

Inside, there was no sawdust in sight. Just stacks of newspapers and junk mail. It was so strewn with "stuff," I could barely see a place to set my tea.

Joe was in no hurry for picture-taking. He talked. Iditarod and dogs. His work for the U.S. Army, recovering crashed planes by dog team. Homesteading at Flat Horn Lake. Plane crashes he'd survived. How he summited Mount McKinley with a team. More dog stories. In another trailer stacked with junk, he showed me slides documenting his stories. Here was living proof, in full Kodachrome color, of his real-life Alaskan adventure.

I'd come north to live out my dream, a narrative that was a pretty close version of what Joe was describing. I was mesmerized, ready to join in.

"Running a team to Nome," Joe said. "No better adventure than that."

"I don't think I'm ready for that."

"Then come take pictures for us!" he challenged.

Now that I could do. I *wanted* to do.

Joe sent me to that year's race manager, Dick Mackey, to discuss getting out on the trail. I met him at the Iditarod headquarters, an office above Teeland's Country Store in Wasilla. Dick had depressing news, suggesting that the Iditarod Trail Committee really didn't want "hitchhikers" on their planes. He sent me

A lack of snow in 1981 forced a change of plans. Instead of the downtown start in Anchorage, organizers arranged for a simple ceremony at Mulcahy Stadium. Each musher and lead dog was introduced, then teams were trucked to Settler's Bay in Wasilla for the start. Here DeeDee Jonrowe, in her second Iditarod, waits her turn at the microphone with her two leaders.

to a local pilot who had volunteered to fly the trail, but that the ITC wouldn't be using. Dr. Von Mitton was a traveling oral surgeon who agreed to fly me if I paid for his gas and oil.

"Okay," I said. "I have $500. Let's see how far that will get us."

The 1981 Iditarod started at Anchorage's Mulcahy Stadium. I had no idea what I was doing, but started

In Nome at my first finisher's banquet, in 1981, I photographed then three-time winner Rick Swenson with his lead dog, Andy. This exceptional dog led Rick to the winner's circle four times. As a newbie, I had no idea who Rick was or how great a musher he was. He was just the guy who won that year's race.

by shooting the mushers and their leaders, with black-and-white film in one camera and color slides in another. I was unsure of just who was whom, what was happening, what photos I should take, and why. But I followed my gut instinct, shooting what looked good and striving to anticipate the action.

Dr. Mitton and I left his home airstrip in his PA-12, a three-seater (another first for me). We had no plan, except to fly the trail and take photos. Several times we overnighted at trailside, outside a checkpoint. We carried our own food and supplies.

While taking pictures of dog teams moving along this beautiful, virgin landscape—I was living the dream. When my $500 ran out, after the halfway point, Dr. Mitton flew me back to Anchorage, and I took a commercial flight to Nome for the finish. I watched as nearly all of Nome turned out to see

Jim Brown was already an official Iditarod photographer when I was asked to join. It was a role we shared from 1982 until 2000. Always helping out the newcomer, Jim often saved me a sleeping place at a checkpoint or a good spot in the finish chute. In this 1980s-era photo, he rests on a snow berm at the Anchorage start. At age 85 in 2000, Jim could not travel the trail any longer. He was a great inspiration.

the first musher arrive, then joined in as the heroic finishers were celebrated at a banquet.

Weeks later, after I'd developed the black-and-white film and got my color slides back, I saw what I thought were some great photos—and a lot of mistakes, too. I made some prints and met with Dorothy Page, an Iditarod Trail Committee board member who also edited the *Iditarod Trail Annual*. This was a yearbook-style publication that Dorothy published as a fundraiser each year. I offered her free use of any of my photos; she was happy to get them.

A few months later I got great news: if I wanted to shoot the next year's race and donate photos again, the ITC would fly me in *their* planes. I could eat with the other volunteers, and sleep where they slept. I would be one of their official photographers. It was a godsend.

In accepting their offer, my life was forever changed . . . and in 1992, it nearly cost me my life. I've made lifelong friends across the state, and the Iditarod helped define my photography career. I was in for the long haul.

A self-timer shot captured this 1981 image of my boyhood best friend Bob Finke and me under the original burled arch finish line in Nome. Bob and I volunteered to help set up the finish by securing 50-gallon barrels and wire fencing along the chute to keep the crowd back.

My first Iditarod volunteer pilot, Dr. Von Mitton, poses with his PA-12 airplane in this 1982 photo on Puntilla Lake at the Rainy Pass checkpoint. Von flew me in this plane for my first eight or so races. He enjoyed the adventure as much as I did, and if his gas, oil and meals were paid for, he was all in.

In preparation for the first Iditarod in 1973, Joe Sr. and Dick Mackey had personally cleared and marked miles of the old Iditarod Trail that had overgrown in Southcentral Alaska. Here, in 1980, I photographed Joe and Dick as they put up a new type of Iditarod sign along the trail near Joe's home in Knik.

THE GREAT ONES: JOE SR. AND MOUNT MCKINLEY

All the preplanning was coming together. It was early April, 1982, about 4:00 A.M. The sky was clear, the air crisp. Denali, or "The Mountain," as Alaskans call Mount McKinley, was jutting out of the earth in its massive form, humbling us below. My lifelong friend, Ron Halsey, and I stood at the edge of a lake near Talkeetna . . . or a swamp. It's hard to tell at that time of year.

We had slept in a truck parked by the side of the road at Mile 131 Parks Highway so we could get a jump on the early light. I'd set up with my Canon F-1 camera on a tripod, a 200mm lens with a polarizer, and a pocket full of film. A couple hundred yards away, Joe Redington, Sr., was commanding his dogs left and right, *gee* and *haw*, with the mountain looming behind them. The early light was just touching its peaks. Gorgeous.

According to plan, Joe Sr. would make several runs around the lake as I took pictures. He'd once told me that he had trained a leader so well, he could use his team to write his signature in the snow using verbal commands. Watching him run his dogs today was a thing of beauty, and I took shot after shot.

Suddenly, as Joe was making a turn on the second run, a sled runner caught and the sled tipped, sending Joe flying over and sideways onto rock-hard packed snow. Naturally, Joe never let go (the number-one rule of dog mushing). But it looked bad. He wasn't moving much, and the dogs were straining to keep going. Ron and I sprinted over.

Joe's hands still clenched the handlebar as the dogs barked and tugged. Blood was streaming down his face and darkening the snow. I panicked, thinking, *This is the FATHER OF THE IDITAROD. What have I done to him, just to get a picture?!* We secured the sled with the snow hook and held tightly as the dogs continued to lunge and Joe composed himself.

"I'm alright," he said. "Nothing to worry about." He urged us to continue, saying he'd just wipe off the blood. Joe knew the importance of good photos and documentation. He was an avid photographer himself, taking thousands of photos in Kodachrome since arriving in Alaska in 1948. But the blood flow didn't let up, so I called it a day.

The photo shoot was Bill Devine's idea. He was one of Joe's closest friends and the artist who designed the official Iditarod logo with the husky head and the capital I. Bill said he'd always wanted to photograph Joe Sr. with Mount McKinley, and suggested I do it instead. We'd set up the rendezvous near a spot that Joe knew would afford a good shot of the Mountain. Joe had slept in his truck that night, too. In the early hours, Ron and I had ridden in Joe's "basket," the dogsled, to reach this perfect location for our shoot, which was now over.

About a week later, the slides arrived back from the Kodak lab, and I saw I had something worthwhile. I took a couple of the best to Alice Puster, *Anchorage Times* photo editor. She offered me $50 to run one. The next Sunday, there it was on the front page, along with my name in the photo credit. I was beaming. I thought I had made it. The paper started getting letters and phone calls from people wanting a print. This was the image that launched my career as a professional.

Timing is everything. We slept in our vehicles to ensure we'd capture the light on the mountain just right as Joe Sr. mushed on the frozen lake.

IDITAROD CHECKPOINTS

■ NORTHERN ROUTE

Checkpoints

ANCHORAGE DISTANCE TO NOME IN MILES	Distance between Checkpoints*	Distance from Anchorage	Distance to Nome
Anchorage to Campbell Airstrip	11	11	964
Willow to Yentna Station	42	53	922
Yentna Station to Skwentna	30	83	892
Skwentna to Finger Lake	40	123	852
Finger Lake to Rainy Pass	30	153	822
Rainy Pass to Rohn	35	188	787
Rohn to Nikolai	75	263	712
Nikolai to McGrath	48	311	664
McGrath to Takotna	18	329	646
Takotna to Ophir	23	352	623
Ophir to Cripple	73	425	550
Cripple to Ruby	70	495	480
Ruby to Galena	50	545	430
Galena to Nulato	37	582	393
Nulato to Kaltag	47	629	346
Kaltag to Unalakleet	85	714	261
Unalakleet to Shaktoolik	40	754	221
Shaktoolik to Koyuk	50	804	171
Koyuk to Elim	48	852	123
Elim to Golovin	28	880	95
Golovin to White Mountain	18	898	77
White Mountain to Safety	55	953	22
Safety to Nome	22	975	0

TOTAL DISTANCE IN MILES   975

* Actual distances can vary depending on weather

■ SOUTHERN ROUTE

Checkpoints

ANCHORAGE DISTANCE TO NOME IN MILES	Distance between Checkpoints*	Distance from Anchorage	Distance to Nome
Ophir to Iditarod	80	432	56
Iditarod to Shageluk	55	487	511
Shageluk to Anvik	25	512	486
Anvik to Grayling	18	530	468
Grayling to Eagle Island	62	592	406
Eagle Island to Kaltag	60	652	346

TOTAL DISTANCE IN MILES   998

* Actual distances can vary depending on weather

The Iditarod as You've Never Seen It

More than a thousand miles of trail. That crosses a lot of country, and all in just one state. Travelling the Iditarod is akin to driving from Miami, Florida, and through four other states before arriving in Baltimore, Maryland. For some small towns and remote villages, it's the only connecting "road" between them. Most of mainland Alaska is referred to as the "Bush," where small communities dot the riverways and coastline. Communities may have a few miles of self-contained roads, but to get there, travel may require a plane or boat, and in winter, snowmachines or dog teams.

Extreme adventurers and sports enthusiasts annually conquer the Iditarod Trail on foot, cross-country skis, or bicycle. But for following the race on the ground, that would be by snowmachine. We find two to five small groups of recreational snowmachiners following the trail each year.

Beyond Willow (the official start line), there are twenty-some checkpoints and villages where a total of perhaps 3,000 people, mostly Native Alaskans, live year-round. At each checkpoint, mushers are required to stop and register with an official time-keeper/checker. The finish line lies in the city of Nome, a veritable metropolis of about 4,000 inhabitants.

The trail's checkpoints are diverse, ranging from a temporary tent camp set up by the Iditarod Trail Committee and manned with fifteen or so volunteers, to villages of a few hundred people who volunteer their community center or school as the checkpoint. In other places, the gold-mining ghost towns, a historical cabin might be used for the checkpoint.

For me, the people in these checkpoints are what make the race special. Some were already living in a particular village when the first race came through in 1973, and today may still be serving as a volunteer. Year after year. Even if they're not volunteering, villagers graciously endure. Imagine your street, covered with snow. Now, in the next week, fifty or sixty dog mushers will pull into town and park their dog teams on your street, each with thirteen to sixteen dogs, straw spread out for each of the dog's beds. That's six hundred and fifty to nearly a *thousand* dogs—howling, barking, eating, peeing, and pooping dogs—twenty-four hours a day for a week straight. The mushers are arriving and leaving at all hours, and volunteers are walking around helping the mushers with

MILE 00 2008 Joyfully, Karen Ramstead joins the group howl at the start line in Anchorage. Meanwhile, volunteers use leashes attached to the sled to add power to Karen's brake.

MILE 00 2006 Mitch Seavey's team leaves the ceremonial start line in downtown Anchorage at 4th Avenue and D Street as the sun rises over the historic Club 25 building.

what they need. Also, trailing behind that whole week, someone (perhaps you) is helping to clean it all up. It takes some pretty amazing people to put up with that each year.

Weather and trail conditions typically change from year to year, so every year is a fresh challenge. While much of the trail is snowy and flat, cutting through black spruce trees, other sections traverse mountain passes, near abandoned gold-rush buildings, and over treeless hills where one can see for miles. The trail follows the frozen Yukon River for many miles. With each trail mile, the landscape changes subtly yet noticeably, moving from one microclimate to the next.

In the early years of the race, and even into the mid-1980s, it wasn't uncommon for a musher to follow a trail that was not properly marked, and end up lost. It still happens today, but rarely. Ahead of the mushers is a team of five or six "trailbreakers" on snowmachines (the Alaskan term for snowmobiles) whose job it is to mark the trail. To do that, each year they plant more than 15,000 wooden survey stakes, attach about 5,000 yards of reflective ribbon, and affix at least 100 new metal reflectors.

The trailbreakers follow the historic Iditarod Trail, a system of trails originally used by Alaska Native travelers and gold-seekers, and officially surveyed in 1911, when gold, mail, passengers, and freight were moved by dog team and horse-drawn wagons between Nome and Seward, Alaska, on Resurrection Bay. Today's snowmachine trailbreakers follow blazes on trees and obvious cleared sections. In areas where

there are no trees, "tripods" often mark the trail year-round.

All that combines to make the Iditarod Trail one of the most challenging, spectacular, unique and foreboding raceways available in modern sporting events in America.

Following is an armchair view of the Iditarod Trail, from start to finish, and an insider's look at the incredibly diverse regions and climate zones it traverses.

NOTE: The mileage markers in this chapter are intended to give the reader a sense of where they are on the trail. Mileage markers from the ceremonial start cover only the 11 miles of Anchorage trail. Mileage for the rest of the trail begins at Mile 0, from the present-day restart at Willow. Due to course changes, the exact milepost numbers of certain trail locations have varied through the years; elsewhere, the trail hasn't changed in a hundred years. Consequently, the present-day trail is no longer located where some of these photos were taken.

MILE .3 2005 Cliff Wang's lead dogs kick up the soft snow laid down the night before on Cordova Street specifically for the Iditarod ceremonial start.

MILE 3.7 2006 Rookie musher Chad Schouweiler avoids a near spill as the trail makes a hairpin turn after crossing a pedestrian bridge over Northern Lights Boulevard.

MILE 4.6 2007 Young Anna Jaeger and friend share muffins with Iditarider Jose Cadiz and musher Rick Casillo along a stretch mushers call the "Muffin Checkpoint," which passes by the backyards of homes on Wesleyan Drive.

MILE 5.3 2011 Spectators who line nearly the entire 11-mile ceremonial start are close enough to give high-fives to mushers. Here, Pete Kaiser and his handler are welcomed as they negotiate the trail near the Alaska Native Medical Center.

MILE 6.2 2010 A team heads down the ramp after crossing busy Tudor Road using the groomed and maintained bike/ski trail overpass.

Willow Lake is Iditarod's starting line on the first Sunday in March. For each musher, the official time clock starts with the word "Go!" From this spot along the Parks Highway, mushers leave the road system and head into the Bush. Warmly dressed fans line up four and five people deep along orange fencing, which disappears as mushers cross the lake. Further on, smaller clusters of race followers settle in at favorite trailside places for an Alaskan version of a tailgate party in the snow. The first two checkpoints, Yentna Station and Skwentna, are lightly populated places that boom with perennial volunteers at this time of the year. Mushers who pause here will load up their plates with mounds of comfort food—a welcoming hallmark for these two checkpoints.

WILLOW RESTART 2006 Handel, a Tim Osmar dog, waits patiently in his dog box in the staging area.

WILLOW RESTART CHUTE 2009 Volunteer start chute controller, Pat Likos (far right) signals Blake Matray's handlers to slowly walk the dogs to the line.

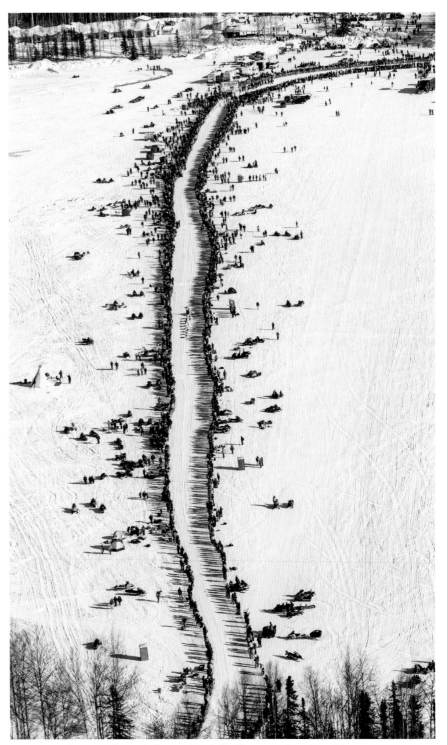

WILLOW RESTART 2007 A Tollef Monson team dog goes airborne in anticipation of the countdown.

MILE .5 2011 Fans on Willow Lake line out for a half-mile to get a clear view of the teams.

WILLOW RESTART 2005 Norwegian race fans wave their country's flag to cheer on their countryman, Robert Sørlie.

MILE 3 2006 Locals make a picnic and spectator event out of the restart as they wave and cheer on Aaron Burmeister on Long Lake.

MILE .5 2010 The Talkeetna Mountains rise in the background as Sebastian Schnuelle's team runs through the gauntlet of race fans on Willow Lake.

MILE 4 2006 Traveling on Long Lake, Doug Swingley's team cruises by the K-9 Fairies, whose mission is to bring merriment to the mushers as they raise awareness for breast cancer.

MILE 4.4 2006 Planes, snowmachines and a truck have brought picnickers out to Long Lake for several hours of watching dogs pass by, among them John Barron's team.

MILE 37 2011 With Mount McKinley and the Alaska Range as a dramatic backdrop, a team heads toward the Yentna checkpoint, following the Yentna River.

MILE 42 2011 Bagged bales of hay mark the sign-in lanes at the first checkpoint, Gabryszak's Yentna Station Roadhouse.

Some would say this mountainous region is the most beautiful in the race, and for that reason, it's a favorite for photographers from all over the world. Dramatic peaks serve as backdrops, and spruce trees thin out as the trail wends up and over snowy Rainy Pass, then descends into the infamous Dalzell Gorge. This portion of the trail—depending on the weather—can induce dread in rookies and veterans alike. The Gorge is legendary for its challenging elevation changes, narrow canyons, switchbacks, and occasional crossings over open, fast-moving water. Beyond it awaits the historic Rohn Roadhouse for a much-needed breather, then onward to the Buffalo Tunnels and the Farewell Burn. Each of those stretches has left mushers with broken sleds and sore bodies . . . and matchless trail stories.

MILE 111 2006 Ramey Smyth leads DeeDee Jonrowe and John Barron in deep, fresh snow on Finger Lake as they near the checkpoint.

MILE 112 2007 As morning breaks and a full moon descends behind the Tordrillo Mountains, Aaron Burmeister's team crosses Finger Lake in a blur.

MILE 112 2013 Volunteers are abuzz as teams check in during the wee hours at the Finger Lake checkpoint. Newer technology "weather ports" have replaced canvas tents as accommodations for race officials.

MILE 112 1999 Old-school canvas wall tents are set up as temporary accommodations for the Finger Lake checkpoint for use by volunteer checkers, veterinarians, and race officials.

MILE 112 2011 As dawn breaks over Carl and Kirsten Dixon's Winterlake Lodge, race officials check in both Judy Currier (left) and Rick Swenson at the Finger Lake checkpoint.

MILE 112 2007 Ray Redington Jr. talks with a Finger Lake checkpoint veterinarian while preparing dog food in his cooker.

MILE 115 2006 Fresh snow covers the trail on Red Lake, just beyond the Finger Lake checkpoint. The next stop for musher Jim Lanier is Rainy Pass.

MILE 123 2011 The Happy River Steps is a notorious series of switchbacks that quickly descend to the Happy River, a stretch that mushers must negotiate with care to avoid sled-busting crashes. This year, Ramey Smyth was able to keep the sled runners down until the very last step.

MILE 123 2013 Four-time Iditarod champion Lance Mackey and team run through the birch and spruce forest of the Happy River Steps.

MILE 142 2006 Airplanes bed down for the night on Puntilla Lake in front of Rainy Pass Lodge. The establishment, owned by the Perrins family, has been the official Rainy Pass checkpoint since the first race in 1973.

MILE 141 2006 A mile from the Rainy Pass checkpoint, Bjornar Anderson traverses a steep embankment onto Puntilla Lake. Situated on the lake, the checkpoint lies below the mountain pass with the same name.

MILE 142 2010 Buckey Winkley keeps his restored 1924 Ford Model T snowmobile at Rainy Pass Lodge, where he lives and works as a big-game guide.

MILE 142 2005 Resting with other mushers and teams on Puntilla Lake, Ed Iten grabs a catnap atop his sled.

MILE 142 2013 Veterinarians examine dogs by headlamp as Kristy and Anna Berington and Rohn Buser teams rest on straw at the Rainy Pass checkpoint.

MILE 142 2013 Leaving the Rainy Pass checkpoint, Jason Mackey's team passes planes and a helicopter parked on Puntilla Lake.

MILE 148 2004
DeeDee Jonrowe runs in the wide Ptarmigan Valley, nearly halfway to Rainy Pass.

MILE 151 2004
With the Alaska Range looming large behind him, Tim Osmar runs along a ridge in Ptarmigan Valley, closing in on Rainy Pass.

MILE 160 2011 Hans Gatt is only yards away from the summit of Rainy Pass, the highest point on the trail at 3,350 feet. The permanent sign was placed by Bob Jones, a dedicated Iditarod fan who has followed the race by snowmachine many times.

MILE 162 2005   Norwegian entrant Kjetil Backen manages the winding, narrow stretch of trail along the Pass Fork of Dalzell Creek, just a few miles beyond the Rainy Pass summit.

MILE 164 2009 After Rick Swenson's dogs took a wrong turn in the willow-choked area of Dalzell Creek's Pass Fork, he found himself breaking trail to return to the main trail as he pursued Paul Gebhardt.

MILE 167 1993 Musher Paul Rupple's headlamp streaks down a level section of Dalzell Creek as the northern lights and stars whirl overhead.

MILE 170 2010 Dave DeCaro's team rounds a corner and heads over an ice bridge deep in the Dalzell Gorge. Beyond him, the peaks of the Alaska Range's Teocalli Mountains are visible.

MILE 170 2010 Encountering an ice bridge, Billy Snodgrass tips his sled and walks it to avoid the steep drop to the open water of Dalzell Creek.

MILE 171 2010 As the trail wends toward the Tatina River, Wattie McDonald maneuvers his sled through spruce trees on a tight stretch in the Dalzell Gorge.

MILE 177 2008 Teams rest on straw in the spruce forest next to the BLM cabin as musher Gene L. Smith arrives at the Rohn checkpoint. During the days of the Iditarod Trail dogsled mail carriers, a roadhouse once stood near here.

MILE 177 2013 From left, volunteers Tina Scheer and Alan Tilling, and local trapper Denny Webber lead Christine Roalofs' team to a parking spot at Rohn. The lone BLM cabin was built in 1939 to shelter stranded pilots. Behind them, the Terra Cotta Mountains may be seen.

MILE 179 1999 Just after leaving the Rohn checkpoint in sub-zero temperatures, Sonny King comes upon shallow, open water on the South Fork of the Kuskokwim River. ▶ Facing page:

Sonny King leaves the sled to lead his dogs through the crossing.

MILE 179 2008 Melissa Owens leaves Rohn on a trail comprised of glare ice and rock. The route will cut into the woods just left of the small island directly ahead, where the local buffalo have created a maze of trails that mushers call the "Buffalo Tunnels." In the background is Egypt Mountain.

MILE 187 2013 Ten miles outside of Rohn, Richie Diehl runs through a burned-out section of trail in the 75-mile span between Rohn and Nikolai. The Terra Cotta Mountains are visible in the distance.

MILE 218 1993 Stemming from a 1978 fire that claimed 1.5 million acres, the Farewell Burn still remains stripped of much of the black spruce trees that once dotted the area.

MILE 189 2005 Jeff Deeter pushes up "The Glacier," which is actually a section where water weeps out of the hillside and freezes into glare ice.

The Iditarod race route forks at Ophir. In odd-numbered years, the trail runs south through the ghost town of Iditarod in an Athabascan region that's also rich in gold-mining history; in even-numbered years, it wends north through Cripple and a series of small Athabascan villages that also warmly support the race by welcoming, checking in, and feeding the mushers. Both routes meet again at Kaltag and continue to Nome.

Because of this north-south variation, during even years, Kaltag (on the last page of this section) is located at Mile 618 of the race; in odd years, it is Mile 641. From Kaltag and beyond, we've keyed the trail location as NR for the Northern Route milepost and SR for the Southern Route, such as "Kaltag NR 618/SR 641."

MILE 252 2008 Nikolai volunteers lead Jerry Sousa's team to a parking area, where they will eat and rest.

MILE 252 2007 At Nikolai, Kevin Morlock, Ben Stamm, and Hernan Maquieira tend to their teams as the dogs rest on temporary straw beds. The wall tent in background acts as a warming area for volunteers.

MILE 252 2007 Mitch Seavey travels upstream on the Kuskokwim River as he approaches the first Native Alaskan village on the trail, Nikolai, where teams rest in the sun.

MILE 277 2006 An unidentified musher travels along a portion of the Kuskokwim River on the 48-mile trail between Nikolai and McGrath.

MILE 300 2006 Traveling together, the Norwegian couple Tove Sørenson and Tore Albrigtsen leave the McGrath checkpoint on the Kuskokwim River. Visible is Takotna Mountain, some 18 trail-miles away and across from the next checkpoint at Takotna.

MILE 300 2009 Replacement sleds await their mushers at the McGrath checkpoint.

MILE 300 2012 Holly Carson, left, and granddaughter Catherine Carson look on as Trent Herbst's dogs rest shortly after their arrival at McGrath.

MILE 311 2012 Ryne Olson wends through a black-spruce forest on the 18-mile overland trail between McGrath and Takotna.

MILE 317 2010 Allen Moore is moments from stopping to check-in at Takotna as volunteers wait for his arrival.

MILE 318 2013 Working in a heavy snowfall, volunteers check in Jason Mackey at Takotna.

MILE 318 2012 Fifteen-year-old Takotna resident Sabrina Anselment pours cold water into a garbage can that has been repurposed as a wood-fired water heater. Mushers who rest in Takotna are treated to the luxury of ready-made hot water.

MILE 318 2007 Refreshed after her twenty-four-hour layover in Takotna, musher Sigrid Ekran gives a high-five to her brother Petter on her way out of the checkpoint.

MILE 332 2008 Between Takotna and Ophir, the trail follows an old gold-mining road for 23 miles.

MILE 339 2008 Warren Palfrey runs his team next to old mining buildings in the Ophir mining district shortly before arriving at the checkpoint.

MILE 341 2007 Cim Smyth checks into Ophir near cabins owned by the Dick and Audra Forsgren family. The Forsgrens have donated use of the buildings since the first race in 1973.

MILE 367 2008 Dr. Jim Lanier mushes his dogs through scrub spruce trees on the swampy overland trail covering 73 miles between Ophir and Cripple.

MILE 414 2012 Trent Herbst closes in on the wall-tent Cripple checkpoint, the halfway point on the Northern Route. Blue straw bags mark parallel parking spaces for resting teams.

MILE 414 2012 Steam rises as white vapor from mushers' dog-food cookers as dogs rest on straw under the northern lights at Cripple. The sleeping and cook tents have been reinforced with plywood by volunteer Jim Paulus and stay up year-round.

MILE 437 1992 Tomas Israelsson negotiates a deep creek ravine by walking his sled down the trail out of Cripple. The logs spanning the ravine were put in place by trailbreakers.

MILE 462 2012 A musher runs in the hills on the mining road along the 70 trail-miles between Cripple and Ruby. A sliver of the Yukon River is visible just below the horizon line in the distance.

MILE 484 2012 Young Vernon Albert watches Anjanette Steer direct her team through the village and up the road as she arrives in the Yukon River village of Ruby.

MILE 484 2010 Parked near the Ruby Bible Church, Paul Gebhardt boots his dogs as he readies to leave the Athabascan village checkpoint of Ruby.

MILE 484 2004 Teams rest along the main street in downtown Ruby near the Community Center checkpoint, the building with a rotunda.

MILE 484.5 2010 Headed out of the Ruby checkpoint at sunset, Dallas Seavey glides down the bank of the Yukon River. This year the Yukon was studded with snow-covered ice blocks pushed up by ice pressure.

MILE 485 2008 The "Rocks" at Ruby are a favorite backdrop for me . . . and many other photographers. Here, Lance Mackey begins his 50-mile flat journey on the Yukon River to the next checkpoint at Galena.

MILE 532 2008 With cut spruce trees marking the trail, Louis Nelson Sr. runs up the bank of the Yukon River nearing the Galena checkpoint.

MILE 487 2006 Just 3 miles into a 134-mile journey on the mind-numbing Yukon River, Tove Sørensen runs headfirst into a ground storm against 30 mph winds.

MILE 534 2014 Eight-year-old volunteer Sable Scotton helps rake away used straw after a musher leaves the Galena checkpoint. The health of the dogs is a main factor in cleaning up used parking areas.

MILE 510 2012 Spruce trees cast long shadows as a team travels a smooth and level trail on the Yukon between Ruby and Galena.

MILE 571 2006 John Baker works his way past houses along the streets of Nulato heading toward the village community center checkpoint.

MILE 559 2002 The cut bank of the Yukon River dwarfs Jeff King on his 37-mile run from Galena to Nulato.

MILE 571 2003 Jim Lanier throws his weight to make a sharp, icy corner in the village of Nulato.

MILE 601 2006 Jeff King uses a ski pole and kicking to help propel the sled forward as he travels through snow drifts on the 47-mile stretch between Nulato and Kaltag.

NOTE: NR stands for northern route milepost (in even-numbered years); SR stands for southern route (in odd-numbered years).
MILE NR 618/SR 641 2008 Mushers share the trail with extreme athletes such as Carl Hutchins of the United Kingdom, competing in a separate event called Iditasport. Here Hutchins is passed by musher Ramey Smyth on the banks of the Yukon as they both arrive at Kaltag at dawn.

MILE NR 618/SR 641 2006 Race judge Rich Bosella directs musher Bob Bundtzen to the parking area outside the community center at Kaltag.

MILE NR 618/SR 641 2008 Youngsters Jamie and Calvin McGinty of Kaltag watch as Aaron Burmeister's dogs eat and rest.

The trail and race derive their names from the gold-rush town of "Iditarod," a once-thriving community that was abandoned nearly a century ago.

In the early part of the 20th century, this area was a hub of gold-mining activity, and massive steamboats were moored along the river's edge as people and goods moved in and out. Seasonally, teams of horses or working dogs transported passengers, freight, mail, and bars of gold to Mile 0 of the Iditarod Trail at Seward, an ice-free port, to waiting ships. Today the Iditarod checkpoint is created with temporary structures on the river ice; remnants of the once-bustling town lie about under snowy mounds. Further on, teams travel through the small, hospitable Athabascan villages of Shageluk, Anvik, and Grayling, before reaching Eagle Island.

MILE 379 2007 Jason Barron and Aliy Zirkle rest their teams at a dilapidated, abandoned cabin on the trail between Ophir and Iditarod. The historic building is known as "Don's Cabin."

MILE 397 2011 A team passes a permanent tripod marker as the trail crosses open tundra through the hills between Ophir and Iditarod.

MILE 419 2007 Just before reaching the Iditarod checkpoint, the snowless trail leaves Martin Buser and team running over bumpy tundra and tussocks.

MILE 420 2011 John Baker's team trots along the trail just outside the Iditarod checkpoint.

MILE 421 1999 Teams are parked on a slough of the Iditarod River, at the site of the historic, gold-rush town of Iditarod, now abandoned. Over 10,000 people traveled through Iditarod during its heyday of 1909–1910.

MILE 421 2011 The river becomes a runway as the planes of fly-in spectators crowd the scene. Ramey Smyth runs past rundown buildings at the ghost town of Iditarod.

MILE 421 2013 Volunteer checkers and helpers, from left, Bob Bell, Kelley VanMeter, and Jim Paulus check in Brent Sass at the Iditarod checkpoint. Straw, Heet, and water buckets are at the ready for each musher.

MILE 476 2009 Ken Anderson takes a sharp turn next to the village store on the road leading to the checkpoint at Shageluk.

MILE 476 2011 Shageluk school kids take an outing to watch Iditarod musher Bruce Linton race through their village.

MILE 476 2011 The daughter of a Shageluk school teacher, Ella Bird Mercer gets a kiss from a Paul Johnson dog that's resting near her school.

MILE 500 2007 Musher Ramy Brooks runs up the bank of the Yukon River and into the village of Anvik, past the Christ Church Anvik and Whitey's Pool Hall.

MILE 498 2007 Ray Redington Jr. skirts down the Yukon River past a rock face as he approaches Anvik.

MILE 501 2005 Mushers' food bags are lined in alphabetical order outside the village community hall checkpoint and "washeteria" while Ken Anderson checks in.

MILE 519 2007 Grayling school kids climb a birch tree to watch the action of Sigrid Ekran's team sleeping in the sun.

MILE 519 2009 Legally blind musher Racheal Scdoris arrives at Grayling as her guide, Tim Osmar, pulls in at the community hall checkpoint beyond her.

MILE 545 2005 A team is dwarfed by the immensity of the Yukon River in the 62 miles between Grayling and Eagle Island.

MILE 581 2009 Teams rest at the remote and temporary tent checkpoint of Eagle Island as Iditarod Air Force volunteer pilot Bob Elliot waits for takeoff on the makeshift runway.

MILE 582 2009 Eagle Island checkpoint volunteer Doug Zirkle prepares a meal in the ice-cave kitchen and pantry. Volunteers sleep in the Alaskan-made "Arctic Oven" heated tents in the background.

MILE 616 2007 Jeff King's team mushes through 35-mph wind and drifting snow on the Yukon River along the 60-mile stretch from Eagle Island to Kaltag.

ESKIMO VILLAGES AND THE COAST

The coastal villages of western Alaska are almost continuously battered by wind. In fact, the name for Unalakleet is translated as "where the east wind blows." From Shaktoolik to Koyuk to Elim, Golovin and White Mountain, it's all the same: Lacking trees, and with few natural barriers, it is nearly impossible to escape the wind, and when a vicious storm is pushing from behind, teams can be pinned down for hours or days. Trail markers are essential for travelers following the trail across the ice. At the Safety checkpoint, an old movie theater building that was moved here from Nome, mushers don their numbered bibs again before running the last 22 miles to Nome.

MILE NR 621/SR 644 2013 Not long after leaving Kaltag, Michelle Phillips leads Josh Cadzow's dogs by her team as he passes in deep snow.

MILE NR 636/SR 659 1991 Susan Butcher runs her team through unavoidable open water on her way from Kaltag to Unalakleet.

MILE NR 649/SR 672 2003 The 85-mile route from Kaltag to Unalakleet, called "The Kaltag Portage," has been in use by Native Alaskans from time immemorial. Here Martin Buser runs in the Tripod Flats area.

MILE NR 667/SR 690 1999 Attempting to balance in icy overflow near the Old Woman shelter cabin, Sonny King prepares to walk his reluctant team through the hazard. Coming from behind, Joe Garnie would pass him within minutes.

MILE NR 668/SR 740 1999 Hans Gatt keeps an eye on Tim Osmar as he leaves the Old Woman shelter cabin to continue the 85-mile trip from Kaltag to Unalakleet.

MILE NR 698/SR 721 2013 Kelly Griffin comes off a finger of the Unalakleet River and onto tundra as sunrise strikes the Whaleback Mountains.

MILE NR 699/SR 722 2007 A team travels on the snowmachine-packed trail, indented from hundreds of years of use, over the windswept tundra and tussocks nearing Unalakleet.

MILE NR 699/SR 722 2013 With the lights of Unalakleet as a beacon, Cim Smyth uses his headlamp to see his team as he negotiates the last hill toward the Bering Sea coast.

MILE NR 700/SR 723 2005 Hans Gatt follows the trail along power lines heading into Unalakleet. This was the only year the trail followed this route, which was changed due to overflow on the normal trail along the Unalakleet River.

MILE NR 703/SR726 2010 A local Unalakleet village dog greets Jason Barron's team as it approaches the check-in area on the Kouwegok Slough at sunrise. The location is known for its fierce winds; snow fences are visible in the background.

MILE NR 703/SR 726 2007 Many Unalakleet villagers turn out on the banks of the Kouwegok Slough at the check-in area to welcome first-place musher Jeff King.

MILE NR 703/SR 726 2002 Unalakleet, an Iñupiaq word meaning "Where the east wind blows," is no joke this year as locals brave the blustery weather to view the teams resting behind berms that block the wind.

MILE NR 704/SR 727 2010 Bruce Linton, with Paul Gebhardt at his heels, runs past beached boats onto Kouwegok Slough ice as they leave Unalakleet.

MILE NR 704/SR 727 2012 Aliy Zirkle's team casts long shadows on the slough as they begin the 40-mile trip from Unalakleet to Shaktoolik.

MILE NR 709/SR 735 2008 Cim Smyth works his way from sea level upward into the Blueberry Hills on his way to Shaktoolik, the not-so-frozen Norton Sound in the background.

MILE NR 728/SR 751 2006 A team runs on a ribbon of snow along the ridge in what locals call "The Foothills" with Besboro Island and the Norton Sound in the distance.

MILE NR 743/SR 766 2009 Avoiding the deep drifts of the blown-in main street, Sonny Lindner follows the trail markers into the village of Shaktoolik, derived from a Unaliq word meaning "scattered things." The dialect is spoken by the Yup'ik people of the Norton Sound area.

MILE NR 743/SR 766 2013 Dressed for the incessant cold and wind, three-year-old Melody Jackson watches teams resting behind a huge snow-berm windbreak at Shaktoolik.

MILE NR 758/SR 781 2009 En route to Koyuk, Jeff King, Hugh Neff, Hans Gatt, and Mitch Seavey wait out Norton Bay 35 mph winds in a shelter cabin on Island Point, located 15 miles out of Shaktoolik.

MILE NR 783/SR 811 2010 Two teams trace the scratched-in trail on Norton Sound sea ice on their way to Koyuk.

MILE NR 776/SR 784 2009 Aaron Burmeister takes on 35 mph headwinds on Norton Sound as he travels the 50 miles between Shaktoolik and Koyuk with no features to block the wind.

MILE NR 792/SR 815 2010 Gerry Willomitzer runs through jumbled sea ice in his approach to the village of Koyuk.

MILE NR 793/SR 816 2010 Koyuk's community center, middle right, serves as the village's checkpoint. Here, teams rest along the road next to the cemetery.

MILE NR 793/SR 816 2008 Martin Koenig grabs a nap with his dogs as they rest in Koyuk.

MILE NR 825/SR 848 2002 Vern Halter and Jon Little travel the bleak trail past summer fish camps of Elim locals at Moses Point.

MILE NR 802/SR 824 2006 Louis Nelson Sr. makes his way along the rocky Norton Sound coastline on the 48-mile trek from Koyuk to Elim.

MILE NR 840/SR 863 2007 Ramy Brooks finds the trail through pressure ridges of sea ice shortly before the Elim checkpoint.

MILE NR 841/SR 864 2010 A group of Elim schoolchildren welcomes Bill Pinkham as he wends through their village toward the checkpoint at the volunteer fire hall.

MILE NR 841/SR 864 2010 Young Anita Jemewouk pets a Bill Pinkham dog resting at the Elim checkpoint.

MILE NR 841/SR 864 2010 With the Fata Morgana phenomenon, commonly known as the inversion effect, the distant hills look like cliffs, as Colleen Robertia leaves the Elim checkpoint.

MILE NR 842/SR 865 2013 With dawn just beginning to crack color into the sky, Pete Kaiser stops the sled so his dogs can relieve themselves before he leaves Elim.

MILE NR 846/SR 869 2010 Sitting behind his sled, Matt Hayashida cruises along the Norton Sound sea coast about 4 miles after leaving the Elim checkpoint.

MILE NR 855/SR 878 2009 Sebastian Schnuelle leads John Baker uphill on the overland trail in the hills on the 28-mile run between Elim and Golovin.

MILE NR 868/SR 891 2007 With a trail barely visible on the Golovin Bay sea ice, John Baker makes his way toward the "non-checkpoint" village of Golovin.

MILE NR 887/SR 910 2014 Joar Leifseth Ulsom, one of five Norwegian teams in the 2014 Iditarod, runs on the Fish River at White Mountain.

MILE NR 887/SR 910 2012 Checkers are on hand for the arrival of Mike Williams Jr. at White Mountain, where musher food bags await.

MILE NR 887/SR 910 2012 Press photographers move in to capture Aliy Zirkle just a few hundred yards after leaving White Mountain. From left are Loren Holmes of the *Alaska Dispatch*, Greg Ritchie, videographer for the web-based Iditarod Insider, and Marc Lester of the *Anchorage Daily News*.

MILE NR 915/SR 938 2004 With snowmachines making one trail indistinguishable from the rest, Jeff King's dogs fan out as they run on the 55-mile trail between White Mountain and Safety.

MILE NR 927/SR 950 2002 Jeff King moves downhill on the trail off of Topkok Hill toward Taylor Lagoon. Cape Nome can be seen in the background in the upper left.

MILE NR 931/SR 954 2013 With a pattern of rock-hard, wind-sculpted snow framing him, Mitch Seavey makes his way on the inland trail along the Bering Sea on Taylor Lagoon between Topkok Hill and Safety.

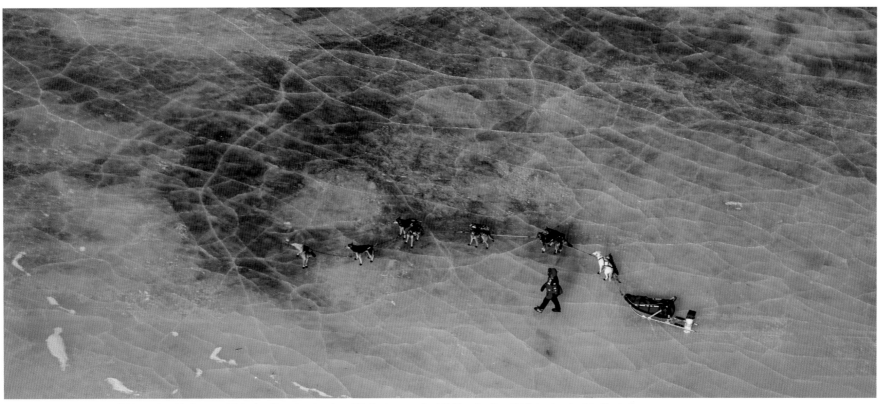

MILE NR 931/SR 954 2007 Without the aid of an established trail on the glare ice of Taylor Lagoon, Paul Gebhardt will walk his leaders back to the trail.

MILE NR 934/SR 957 2013 Mushing on the inside of the Bering Sea beach past a tumbledown cabin, Aliy Zirkle heads for Safety.

END OF THE TRAIL—NOME

The cheering for the frontrunner starts as soon as the team moves off the sea ice and heads down Nome's Front Street. Hooting, shouting, clapping, ringing cowbells, the people are delirious with anticipation . . . and have perhaps visited some of Nome's famed watering holes while they were waiting. The scene near the carved burled arch is as jammed as Times Square on New Year's Eve, with state, national, and international media jockeying for the best shots and a few words from the champion. Often the arriving musher ignores all the microphones and heads straight for his or her leader, kneels, and offers a heartfelt thank you. Days later, at the finishers' banquet, mushers and top dogs are honored with cash prizes, gold nuggets, and other awards. Nomeites will tell you that March itself is a month-long party.

MILE NR 942/SR 965 2004 Jacob Lysyshyn approaches the old "Nome-O-Rama" movie theater building that serves as the Safety checkpoint. The repurposed building was trucked out from Nome after the Safety Roadhouse burned.

MILE NR 960/SR 983 2012 After driving their cars out some 4 miles, local Nome residents line the trail braving 20 mph wind to witness Dallas Seavey approach his finish. Seavey would become the youngest musher to win the Iditarod.

MILE NR 959/SR 982 2013 Kristy Berington glides past a driftwood trail marker and summer fish camps at the area known as Farley's Camp. The Nome finish line lies only 5 miles away.

MILE NR 962/SR985 2006 Within the city limits of Nome, Aliy Zirkle mushes past pressure ridges of the frozen Bering Sea as she nears the sea-wall ramp leading to Front Street.

MILE NR 963/SR 986 2009 Well-wishers greet Sebastian Schnuelle from the road berm that follows the trail the last few miles to Front Street.

MILE NR 963/SR 986 2010 Nearing the finish line, rookie musher Jane Faulkner runs past Nome welcome signs on the sea ice as spectators watch from above.

MILE NR 963/SR 986 2010 Jamaican musher Newton Marshall proudly bears his country's flag as he follows the snow ramp from the sea ice to Nome's Front Street for the final few tenths of a mile to the finish.

MILE NRY 964/SR 987 2010 On pavement, Blake Freking mushes the final blocks of Front Street toward the finish line.

MILE NR 964/SR 987 2014 Justin Savidis lifts Louisa Mae for a canine version of a high five on the Burled Arch, a tradition that he's carried on each year to honor the most exceptional dog in his team for that year.

MILE NR 964/SR 987 2008 Kids and dogs. Dogs and kids. Seven-year-old Ashlann Kowchee of Nome embraces a DeeDee Jonrowe dog in the finish chute.

MILE NR 964/SR 987 2008 DeeDee Jonrowe signs her autograph onto a local kid's jacket at the finish line in Nome.

MILE NR 964/SR 987 2013 Paige Drobny runs up the finish chute as the Widow's Lamp hangs from the burled arch. The lamp is lit at the start of the race and stays lit until the last musher reaches Nome.

MILE NR 964/SR 987 2014 The grandson of race founder Joe Redington Sr., Ray Redington Jr. claimed a spot in the top ten for the 2014 Iditarod, finishing 8th during a year in which former champions were among the many who scratched.

3

The Superstars . . . and Their Mushers

The Iditarod is all about the dogs. Every musher will tell you: "I'm just the coach, the dogs are the *real* athletes."

On the trail, I've seen those mushers putting their dogs first, feeding them, massaging wrists, applying ointment, and getting the team comfortably bedded down before eating or sleeping themselves. The dogs' meals and snacks are monitored for the fat, protein, and moisture that will keep them optimally fueled for mile after mile. And all along the route, teams are treated royally by volunteer veterinarians, pilots, dog handlers, checkers—everyone who comes in contact with them.

These sled dogs have been bred to run, and run they do. They do it so well that the U.S. government has made studies of Iditarod dogs' physical stamina and high-performance metabolism. That data was consequently used to modify how U.S. military dogs are trained and fed.

Likewise, the mushers have to be in shape to endure the miles, able to handle a schedule that's short on sleep and long on cold stretches of standing and riding, followed by bouts of frantic activity.

Mushers come from all walks of life. Women and men on an equal footing.

Karin Hendrickson gets a smooch from Cutter at Takotna, 2012.

There's the professional dog musher, who enjoys the outdoor adventure, farm-type lifestyle. There are those who simply love dogs and the idea of winter traveling and camping. And there are those adventure seekers who just want to add the Iditarod Trail to their list of conquests.

Winning the Iditarod takes a great dog team and a very skilled, smart, and savvy dog musher who knows his or her dogs, the trail, and competitive strategy. (A rookie has not won the Iditarod except in the first two races.) Mushers hand-pick each dog in the team, and their intuitive relationship grows deeper during the miles of solitude. They often speak of the profound gratitude they feel toward their teammates at the finish line, dropping to their knees to show affectionate appreciation right there in the chute.

I've enjoyed getting to know the mushers and their dogs over the years, watching the veterans debut new innovations, noting when someone is moving up the ranks, along for the celebration when a repeat champion does it again. In this portrait gallery, I've attempted to capture the personalities of and feeling between the athletes and their coaches.

Mikhail Telpin dog, 2013

Hans Gatt, 2006

Joseph—Gerry Willomitzer dog, 2009

Joe Redington Sr., 1997

Brownie—Cim Smyth dog, 2008

Sonny Lindner, 2007

Scorpio—Curtis Wayne dog, 2008

Rick Swenson, 1999

Steven and Shy—Bill Hall lead dogs, 1999

Clint Warnke, 2007

Aberdeen and Chase—Karin Hendrickson dogs, 2011

Terry Adkins, 1982

Cleavage—Billy Snodgrass dog, 2011

Mike Williams Jr., 2012

Willow—DeeDee Jonrowe dog, 2013

SUPERSTARS

Charlie Boulding, 2005

Jane—Charlie Boulding dog, 2003

Biscuit—Aliy Zirkle dog, 2009

Aliy Zirkle, 2010

SUPERSTARS

Sebastian Schnuelle cuddles with Gas and Diesel at Takotna, 2009.

Guetknecht, left, and Elwood—Jodi Bailey's energetic leaders cross Long Lake, 2011.

Martin Buser, snacking his team at Unalakleet, 2013.

Justin Savidis takes a deserved rest with Twig, in foreground, and her son, Fritz, at Iditarod, 2013.

SUPERSTARS

Lance Mackey with Larry, the Golden Harness winner, Nome, 2007.   Susan Butcher and puppy, 1989.

Hag—Paul Gebhardt dog, 2010

Paul Gebhardt peers into the dark on Finger Lake, 2012.

Joe Garnie, 2008

Joe Garnie dog, 1999

Robert Sørlie thanks his leader after arriving in Nome, 2007.

Sven Haltmann, 2010

McLeod—Sven Haltmann dog, 2010

SUPERSTARS

Fender—a John Baker dog rests in the sun at Takotna, 2011.

John Baker, 2007

Kristy Berington, 2010

Jonah—Kristy Berington dog, 2010

Melanie Gould, 2002

Melanie Gould dog, 2002

Scamper—Robert Nelson Jr. dog, 2010

Robert Nelson Jr., 2009

SUPERSTARS

Louis Nelson Sr., 2006

Rambo—Louis Nelson Sr. dog, 2007

Norman—Pete Kaiser dog, 2010

Jeff King with Salem, the Golden Harness winner, Nome, 2006.

4

Behind the Clipboard

When I think about what it takes to make the Iditarod happen, I'm blown away. I shake my head, wondering, *How do they ever pull this off?*

In the 1980s, when I first volunteered, preparations looked more like a cat-herding exercise, and I'm still amazed that those early races came off so well. Back when communications were limited and there were fewer volunteers, things could and did go wrong.

Sometimes mushers had to scrounge a meal for themselves or their dogs, because they'd arrived at the checkpoint before their food bags did. So they'd ask other mushers for a favor or open the food bag of someone who'd scratched. And a change-up in food could be problematic for their dogs.

Occasionally a musher showed up at a checkpoint unexpectedly, while the checker had stepped away or was grabbing a nap. So the musher, who is required to sign in on the clipboard, would have to park the team and knock on a stranger's cabin door, wake them, and ask where the checker lived.

Without the communications we have today, nobody knew if a team was going to arrive at any given checkpoint within the hour, in the next five hours, or even the same day. Some villages had only one community phone. The ham radio operators and word of mouth—from pilots, mushers, and passing snowmachiners—served the purpose. Sometimes an official had to wait hours to sort out a garbled ham radio message that a certain musher had checked in. The good ol' days, they call those.

Logistics are easier now, especially after more

▲ A small army of volunteers and a very big space is required for the work surrounding the food-bag drop. Weeks before the race, each musher receives a quantity of durable bags, each preprinted with a checkpoint name. The bags are filled with food (human and canine), supplies, and any other anticipated need, then mushers label each bag with their name and return them to the warehouse. Volunteers sort the bags by checkpoint before Iditarod Air Force volunteer pilots or USPS mail planes fly them out.

than four decades of practice. Iditarod also enjoys an influx of eager volunteers, ready for a lifetime adventure, and the advent of modern technology has streamlined the hiccups of communications. At the checkpoints and in between, Bush-dwellers and race volunteers often have access to internet service, cell and satellite phones, FAX machines, or even simple

walkie-talkies. The Iditarod Air Force planes are equipped with GPS.

The dogsleds themselves are outfitted with GPS trackers that transmit signals for officials as well as fans who sign up for Iditarod insider service through the Iditarod.com website. (For a fee, race followers can go online to watch icons representing the trail locations of each musher, view webcam action captured at checkpoints, and enjoy video interviews with the mushers during the race.)

Still, some things haven't changed. The volunteer Iditarod Air Force typically uses Cessna 180 and 185 airplanes, which can carry four people, including the pilot. Without the seats they can haul a good amount for a payload, about 1,100 pounds. The 180 can hold three to five bales of straw in the plane, along with another three or four bags holding the musher's food and dog food, HEET, or other supplies. You figure each checkpoint gets a bale of straw per musher, with the average race of sixty competing mushers, it takes some forty to sixty trips to equip just one checkpoint, such as Rainy Pass, about forty-five minutes from the staging area in Willow.

Prior to and once the supplies arrive at a checkpoint, the unsung volunteers in the villages and checkpoints really make the Iditarod work. Sorting supplies, finding accommodations for the out-of-town volunteers, erecting tents, readying the community center, hauling and chopping firewood, cooking food, marking the trail into and out of town, transporting dropped dogs to the airstrip to fly out. Readying a checkpoint amounts to creating a temporary small community. I am so impressed with the unselfish and unending work that the volunteers do. This could only happen in Alaska.

Following is just a peek into some of the backstage activities I've chronicled over the years.

▲ ▶ Straw bales are bagged for delivery to the checkpoints. They'll be waiting for the teams when they arrive, ready to break into warm, temporary beds for weary dogs . . . and the occasional musher.

▶ Two weeks before the 2009 Iditarod, volunteer Iditarod Air Force pilot John Norris squeaks a cumbersome straw bale through his Cessna 180 door at the Willow airport as he loads up for a thirty-minute flight to Finger Lake. About four straw bales can fit into one of these planes along with smaller musher food bags. It will take about forty-five trips in the 180 to get all the necessary supplies into the Finger Lake checkpoint.

▶ A cardiologist by day, volunteer pilot Dr. Bill Mayer taxis his Cessna 185, filled to the brim, for a forty-five-minute, one-way flight to Rainy Pass in 2013. The Cessna 185 can handle a 1,100-pound payload. The Iditarod Air force is a dedicated group of more than two dozen private pilots, most of whom are not full-time pilots. They donate their time and the air-miles on their personal aircraft. The average Iditarod pilot in 2013 had been volunteering for more than twenty years.

▼ At 7:11 A.M. on the 2013 ceremonial start day, Iditarod Executive Director Stan Hooley is on the cell phone as he surveys the freshly laid snow at the downtown Anchorage start area, 4th Avenue and D Street. The Municipality of Anchorage uses snow-moving equipment overnight to deliver snow back onto the urban streets that the teams will travel.

▶ ▼ Finger Lake 2012—Volunteer Mark Green of Canton, Ohio, shovels dog poop and food remnants from a team that recently departed as Race Judge Mark Lindstrom surveys the dog-lot parking area on the lake. Volunteers keep the parking areas clean for the health of dogs who'll park there next. Clean-up also prevents polluting the lake, used by Winterlake Lodge.

▲ ◄ A handful of the hundreds of 2013 Anchorage start volunteers quickly smooth out tracks caused by vehicle traffic at 4th Avenue and A Street. Vehicles are allowed to cross the 4th Avenue trail during the two-minute intervals between each team's departure, then volunteers jump in to smooth the trail before the next musher comes along.

▲ Nikolai 2005—From left, Ramy Brooks, DeeDee Jonrowe, and John Baker nap in their long-johns on mats laid out on the school gym floor. Top mushers get an average of only four non-consecutive hours of sleep during any twenty-four-hour period as they run. Even with two mandatory eight-hour layovers and one twenty-four-hour layover, contending mushers will sleep an average of only thirty-six hours during the entire nine or ten days from Willow to Nome.

◄ Nikolai 2008—Dropped dogs are loaded into a Peninsula Airways caravan airplane for a ride back to Anchorage by the race sponsor. A musher is only as fast as the slowest dog, so dogs can be dropped from the team for any reason, which can include sore wrists, sickness, fatigue, or simply that the musher feels the dog's head is not in the game any longer. No new dogs can be added.

▲ Rainy Pass 2012—Veterinarian Dr. George Stroberg and musher Kristy Berington examine a dog by headlamp. More than fifty veterinarians volunteer their time and experience each year, and most do it, as Dr. Stroberg says, for "the love of these super-athlete animals." Many vets come back year after year from all over the Lower 48 states and abroad.

◀ After greeting arriving teams for many hours, race judge Art Church gets a catnap inside the community hall. Nearby is a dropped dog that developed an issue requiring that he stay indoors until transport.

▼◀ Nikolai 2013—Village resident and volunteer checker Daryl Petruska adds a spruce log to the hot-water fire. Mushers can help themselves to the hot water as they make dog food. Mushers appreciate villagers who haul water and keep it hot and close to the dog-parking area, as it saves so much time and effort.

▼ McGrath 2011—In the logistics room, chief pilot Bert Hanson and support volunteer Nan Llewellyn go over the tracking board for the day's flights. A volunteer pilot must be willing to fly people, dogs, fuel, or nearly any needed supplies to any given checkpoint, but only if the pilot feels the weather is safe to do so.

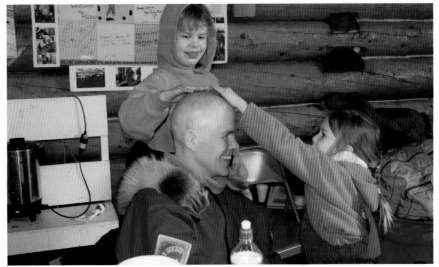

▲ ▲ Takotna 2006—Jan Newton, longtime head of the village checkpoint, stops for a photo after fixing and delivering another dinner to mushers sitting behind her. Jan has since passed away, but Takotna is still known for its great hospitality and food, especially its pies, leading many mushers to take their mandatory twenty-four-hour layover there.

▲ Eagle Island 2009—Volunteer checker and former musher Jim Gallea acts as an anchor/pivot point as pilot Bruce Moroney makes a 180-degree turn with his Cessna 185. This method is often used to help a pilot turn the plane sharply on narrow runways when the wind or snow conditions prohibit such a turn.

◄ Airborne near McGrath 2008—Cory, a dropped dog, leans over volunteer pilot Danny Davidson's shoulder to get a better view during his ten-minute flight from Takotna to McGrath. Once a small plane gets into the air, dropped dogs usually lie quietly on the floor.

▲ ▲ Ruby 2010—Maureen Chrysler, a member of the canine drug-testing team (affectionately known as the P Team) catches a urine sample from Spit, one of Bill Pinkham's dogs. The dogs are randomly tested during the race for illegal, performance-enhancing drugs. Newer rules require mushers to perform a drug test at the end of the trail as well.

▲ Ruby 2006—The daughters of four-time Iditarod champion Susan Butcher, Tekla, left, and Chisana caress their mother's head in the community hall checkpoint. After retiring from the sport, and while battling with cancer, Butcher wanted to give her girls a firsthand glimpse of how special the Iditarod was to her. She passed away later that year.

▲▲Ruby 2012—John Baker gears up after a nap while Jake Berkowitz snoozes on the counter and another musher rests on the floor at a building designated exclusively for mushers. A warm and quiet place for naps and drying gear is not always readily available elsewhere. According to race rules, such a building has to be accessible to every musher; not all checkpoints have such accommodations.

▲ Anvik 2011—Colorful and encouraging posters for the mushers adorn the community center walls. Volunteers including checkers, communications people, veterinarians and the designated Teacher on the Trail grab dinner during a lull in the action. Though every checkpoint is going 24/7, as the checkpoints get closer to Nome, teams are more spread out allowing time for volunteers to enjoy each other and their surroundings.

▶ Kaltag 2010—A Pete Kaiser dog greets volunteer veterinarian Doug Marks, as he reads over remarks from vets at earlier checkpoints in Kaiser's Vet Book. This book is mandatory gear that a musher must present when checking in at each checkpoint. It serves as a diary of the dogs' health throughout the race so vets along the route can monitor any problems. Each dog can be identified quickly by a tag on its collar with the musher's starting number and a letter.

◄ Unalakleet 2013—Borrowing a portion of hangar space from Peninsula Airways (PenAir), Race Manager and Marshal Mark Nordman, left, talks logistics on the phone while volunteer coordinator Teri Paton, middle, coordinates the next day's veterinarian flight moves with Chief Veterinarian Stu Nelson. Every day seems to be a logistical nightmare . . . but it gets done.

◄ Koyuk 2010—Local seven- and eight-year-olds help volunteer checker Brad VanMeter clear Sebastian Schnuelle's used straw from the village's main street. The straw in most checkpoints is either burned or hauled to the local landfill.

◄▼ White Mountain 2012—Working from the village city hall and library, volunteer Communication Specialist Janis Young sends a message to race headquarters in Nome. At nearly all checkpoints, the communications people, or comms, are the main hub of activity. Press, locals, vets, and checkers—all needing information—rely on them to get news out or in. Depending on the checkpoint location, comms use a variety of methods: email, telephone, fax, satellite phone, or pagers.

► Nome 2012—Dropped dogs, their leashes clipped to the plane floor for safety, are anxious to disembark once Iditarod volunteer pilot Jerry Wortley lands in Nome.

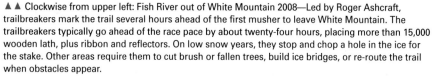

▲ ▲ Clockwise from upper left: Fish River out of White Mountain 2008—Led by Roger Ashcraft, trailbreakers mark the trail several hours ahead of the first musher to leave White Mountain. The trailbreakers typically go ahead of the race pace by about twenty-four hours, placing more than 15,000 wooden lath, plus ribbon and reflectors. On low snow years, they stop and chop a hole in the ice for the stake. Other areas require them to cut brush or fallen trees, build ice bridges, or re-route the trail when obstacles appear.

Nome 2008—An aerial view shows the Nome dog lot where the dogs live after the race before flying home. The dogs here are cared for by their musher, family members, and handlers while access to the dog lot is closely monitored by volunteers. The shipping containers shown here hold dog food, straw, musher sleds, and other supplies.

Nome Airport 2012—Alaska Airlines "Dog Squad" personnel Rick Jabusch and Gerry Bee push a load of dog crates into the cargo bay of a Boeing 737-400 aircraft for the ninety-minute flight back to Anchorage. As many as twenty-seven dog crates can fit, safely strapped and netted into place.

Nome 2004—A Rick Swenson dog curls warmly in straw in a bread box bed. After reaching Nome, the dogs typically stay in the dog lot for two or three days before flying back to Anchorage or Fairbanks.

5

I Have No Dogsled

That's right: I'm not a musher, I don't own a dogsled, nor do I *want* to travel a thousand miles by dogsled. So for me, there are two basic options for traveling the trail in winter: airplane or snowmachine. I use both options as I look for the best opportunities to get unique photos and show the race for what it really is. But my main mode of transportation is the airplane.

Through the years, I've flown with many safe, talented, fun, and energetic pilots whose main responsibility it was to fly me, among them Dr. Von Mitton, Sam Maxwell, and Danny Davidson. Likewise, when my dedicated pilot was not available, I've been fortunate to fly with talented members of the volunteer Iditarod Air Force. Although I remain a volunteer, the deal I have with the Iditarod Trail Committee requires me to be mobile, to stay on the go finding great photos. I prefer not to be stuck in a checkpoint, waiting for a plane.

Instead I sometimes find myself stuck in a checkpoint, waiting for a change in the weather so the plane can leave. There's a saying, "When you have time to spare, go by air." I used to be anxious when I was grounded by weather, thinking I was missing many opportunities. Although I agreed that the pilot knows best, often I'd try to persuade him to fly. *Not a good idea.* Now I know that there's almost always something to photograph wherever I am.

▲ 1994 A self-portrait with pilot Sam Maxwell in the cockpit of his 180.

▼ 1993 Riding behind Barry Stanley near the Gorge. I usually stand on the sled.

I love flying along the route and seeing these centipede-looking teams crawling on the snow and ice. If I spot a unique trail situation that should be photographed from land, we land on a river, swamp, lake, or sea ice between checkpoints, and I'll hike or snowshoe a mile or more to the location. I enjoy these forays in the wilderness. It takes some mushers by surprise, when they see me on the trail miles from any checkpoint with no plane or snowmachine around. They wonder where I came from.

Traveling by Bush plane during winter in Alaska is an adventure in itself. The plane needs to be "put to bed" at night—tied down, wing and engine covers put on, and engine plugged in. And likewise, readied in the morning. I try to help my pilot do all these chores when I can. And then there's packing and unpacking the plane with all our gear and lugging it on our backs, a sled, or snowmachine to where we're staying.

To get out of the checkpoints for trail shots and get to places that aren't reachable by plane, I go by snowmachine. I may rent or borrow snowmachines in many of the village checkpoints to get back up or down the trail a few miles. My favorite section of trail, one I try to cover every year, is the thirty-five mile stretch from the Rainy Pass checkpoint over the Alaska Range to Rohn. The mountains, valleys, and wildlife are spectacular.

DIGGING OUT AT RAINY PASS

My reading glasses fell off and sank in the powder snow as I bent over, wild and desperately hand-digging the snowmachine ski out of a hole. We had gone off the packed trail and into the seemingly bottomless snow in an unsuccessful attempt to pass Iditarod musher Jeff King. Fortunately I quickly found the glasses, and returned to my digging so I could get back to photographing dog teams.

Bundled against the cold, it doesn't take long before one begins to sweat, even at 15°F—at least I thought it was above zero—and that should be avoided. My guide and snowmachine driver, Steve

▶ Steve Perrins II and a videographer dig out our stuck machine after a failed attempt to pass a team in deep snow off the trail.

▼ This is the shot I envisioned of Paul Gebhardt while riding the snowmachine and scanning for the "prime shot."

Perrins II, and I had left the Rainy Pass Lodge some two hours and 12 miles ago.

Several of the top mushers had discreetly informed me that they would be leaving the checkpoint in the next hour or so, so I got ready, too. If a few were leaving, I knew that a trainload of the top teams would soon follow.

I had conceived of a plan a month ago, and it actually seemed to be coming together. I wanted to travel by snowmachine on the 18 miles between the lodge and the Rainy Pass summit during daylight hours. I'd shoot more during the evening on the summit and spend the night at Steve's nearby hunting cabin. I'd planned to pause along the way to photograph these top mushers on my never-ending quest to get that elusive, perfect Iditarod image, one that might someday grace the cover of a magazine or land in a brochure or textbook.

Each year, I work hard to find what I call a "prime spot," then wait there for a musher to come by and complete the picture. The prime spot could be a place that juxtaposes the small musher and team with some spectacular scenery that would simply *scream* "remote Alaska." Or it might be where the trail snakes through a treacherous area, or it could simply be a place I have never photographed in all these years.

When necessary, I pass some of the teams as I travel, shooting them from behind, in front, near, and far away. Wide angle and telephoto. Anything to get a variety of images in my pursuit of that one elusive image. It really doesn't matter to me what dog musher is in the photo. It's all about the "prime spot."

▼ After shooting the main shot, we hurried past Paul, stopped the machine, and I stood on the seat to get this higher angle.

TRAVELING LESSONS

- **WHEN riding on a toboggan sled behind a snowmachine, always face backwards.**
- **WHEN hand-propping an airplane, always stand BEHIND the prop, not in front.**
- **NEVER fly in a small plane that does not have a shoulder harness for you.**
- **BUSH airplanes are made of lightweight and very expensive parts which can bend or break more easily than a car. Always ask the pilot if he'd like to close the door himself.**
- **BE CAREFUL what you grab onto when getting in or out. If you're not sure, ask the pilot lest something get broken and be very expensive to replace.**
- **PACK your gear first thing after waking so that you'll be ready to go when the plane comes. (More than once, the plane came, I was not ready, and they couldn't wait.)**
- **WHEN travelling in the Bush, always have a handheld air-to-ground radio or SAT phone, with fresh batteries and the correct area frequencies (and/or contact phone numbers), and know how to use it.**

I was sitting comfortably behind Steve riding tandem down the trail at 15 mph while constantly scanning the area for a prime spot. Ahead was a musher going about 6 mph, so we left the trail well behind him and rejoined the trail well ahead, to avoid spooking the dogs. Meanwhile, I kept up my survey for a spot, not wanting to waste the opportunity of a musher at hand. About ten minutes later, with the musher further and further behind us, I spotted it.

Off to our right was a pretty picture of some spindly willows, a few still bearing red leaves from autumn, poking starkly through the powdery snow; to my left the landscape looked stark, yet eerily inviting. I tapped Steve on the shoulder and spoke loudly into his ear, directing him to swing around and park well behind those willows.

I surveyed the sight from this new angle. I could envision the musher in the frame broadside, the sun peeking over the mountain and burning its way through the low clouds, combined with those beautifully graphic, spindly willows. *This'll make a decent image*, I thought. *Now if only the musher would get here.*

In dog mushing, there are no guarantees. He may be coming; he may have stopped to snack his dogs; he may have encountered a bootie problem. Still, I needed to behave as if he were about to arrive, so I hurried to set up. The right lens and filter combo and the correct exposure settings. And then the wait.

Even though I'd done this countless times and would again, the adrenaline began to torrent through me. I was excited about getting a great image; scared that I'd blow it somehow.

I asked Steve to turn the machine around and face it down the trail, in the direction we'd go as soon as the musher passed. We'd be jumping on and hurrying past him for the next good spot.

As I went into "auto-photog" mode, confirming that I had the gear I needed, Steve kept his eye on the trail and horizon. In a dog race, when you advise someone that a team is coming, you just say, "Dog team." That's all. You don't say "Here he comes" or "There he is." It's always "Dog team." In my own race, I hurried to prepare before he said those words.

In "auto-photog mode" and in less than a minute, I removed the 24-105mm lens that is always on one of my Canon camera bodies and changed it for an even wider angle lens, a 17-40mm. It was a backlit shot, so I knew I'd need a special split-neutral density filter to bring the bright sunlit clouds into the proper exposure range. I pulled that special filter holder from one of the twenty pockets in my vest, removed the lens hood, and screwed the holder onto the lens in a couple automatic moves. Then I got the split-neutral density filter from yet another pocket and slid it in place.

I knelt down for what I thought would be the best angle and guesstimated the proper exposure. I knew I wanted both the foreground willows and the background mountains all in focus—so I needed decent depth of field. I chose f/11 for that and figured a 1/250 shutter speed might be the right combo at 400 ISO. I shot one frame and then looked at the image and its histogram (the bell-curve data that shows exposure) and saw that the image was too light. I adjusted the shutter speed, shot another test, and said it's good. I really liked the composition of this shot (the art of photography) and I saw from the histogram that the exposure was correct (the science aspect), so at last I felt ready.

I double-checked more camera settings and confirmed that a) the battery had sufficient juice; b) I wouldn't run out of frames on the card—there were more than 220 frames left shooting in RAW on the 16 GB card; and c) the motor drive was set to "high," so five frames per second would fly onto the card, capturing the musher all the way through the composed scene. Because I had time and because I am always greedy for more photos, I gathered my second camera body and put on a long telephoto lens.

I had my back to the trail when Steve called out "Dog team!" The adrenaline began rushing even faster. I stood on the snowmachine seat to get the telephoto shot. As soon as I got a dozen shots off, I stepped down, left the telephoto lens on the seat and dropped to my knees for "the" shot.

The musher was Paul Gebhardt. As I framed the image, I noticed that he was in a red parka. *Nice touch*, I thought. I took a quick shot just before he got into the frame to do one double-check of the exposure, in case things had changed in the past few minutes. He got closer without saying a word or acknowledging us. As the team approached the perfect spot, I pressed the shutter and it began its five-frames-per-second repetition. In three seconds, he was out of the frame. I didn't pay too much attention, but slung both cameras on my shoulders as Steve was starting the machine.

We passed him right away and sped to another spot I liked. I had just enough time to stand on the seat for a higher angle as he passed us. We let him go in anticipation of some other teams and to avoid passing him too many times. We continued toward the pass, and I grabbed a few more photos of other teams, but the biggest time-consumer was digging out the snowmachine *two* more times.

I am not *gonna do this again next year*, I was thinking as we dug. I'd never been stuck so many times in one day. Night was closing in, and I had wanted to get to the top while there was still light. Later, at the summit, I was rewarded with a night shot that I felt was one of my best Iditarod shots ever. It was one of the most trying, yet productive days of my trail life, and I was thankful.

That night at the cabin, the adventure continued at zero degrees. The shelter was not meant for winter use, and the missing chinking between the logs let the 10-mph wind have its way. The small woodstove kept at least a portion of the cabin above freezing. For sake of weight, I had brought my lighter-weight sleeping

▲ Packing up in a below-zero windy morning outside the Rainy Pass Lake hunting cabin, readying for the ride to Rohn.

bag. I knew I'd regret that decision in the early morning hours. It would be a cold night's sleep, if I slept at all.

Steve made a warm dinner and used the satellite phone to call the lodge and let them know we were okay. I had already placed my Cabela's winter boots and gloves above the stove, so any dampness would evaporate in the warm drafts. I took the batteries and flash cards out of my cold-soaked cameras and ate as I downloaded the cards to my laptop. The cameras, I placed into plastic bags before I brought them inside to avoid condensation and put them in the heat above the stove. Then it was time to prepare my sleeping area. I put five chemical hand-warmers inside the lightweight bag, then used my heavyweight parka as another blanket, and put tomorrow's clothes inside the bag with me . . . along with a few camera batteries.

Because the race goes on 24/7, we knew that the majority of the mushers would pass us as we

slept. We still had 18 miles to travel by snowmachine through the famous Dalzell Gorge, where we would shoot more teams, if there were anymore heading our way by then, and on to the Rohn checkpoint. Steve stoked the stove one final time as we crawled into our bags.

I woke up chilled but not cold. The chemical hand-warmers had done a decent job keeping me from freezing through the -5°F night. There was snow on the cabin floor. The wind had driven it through the gaps in the logs and through the cracks of a door that wouldn't close. Last night's water was frozen in its pan. Indeed the small stove had not held its last stoking as long as we had hoped. Steve got out of his bag first and started a new fire to take the chill off. Another day on the Iditarod lay ahead.

Whoomph!! The prop grabbed the snow and the Super Cub tilted slightly down and to the left as it came to a stop in the powdery white stuff. A puff of crystals made a small cloud in the air. I was watching and photographing from a distance in 1997 as my pilot, Sam Maxwell, was making a landing in Ptarmigan Valley between the Rainy Pass and Rohn checkpoints. The landing had looked fine, until toward the end of his roll-out, when the plane slowly and effortlessly sank in the fluffy, fresh snow. The Super Cub did not flip or even seem that off-kilter, but nonetheless, Barry Stanley and I immediately rode over to check.

Nonchalantly, Sam stepped out of the plane, sank to his knees and said, "Well, that happened."

A few hours ago, back at the checkpoint at Rainy Pass Lodge, Sam, Barry, and I had devised an on-the-fly plan. It was a sunny and fairly warm late afternoon. I wanted to take full advantage of the light, location, and dog teams, and travel the trail some 10 to 12 miles to make some photos of the top teams up in Ptarmigan Valley. It was too late in the day to make the trip over the pass by snowmachine before dark, so we planned for Barry to tow me behind his snowmachine as I stood on the back of a Fold-A-Sled, something we've done before. Then Sam would come up a few hours later, pick me up for a flight over to Rohn, arriving before dark. Sam would spend the night at Rohn; Barry would make the trip back to the lodge on his own. The one concern of Sam's was having enough room to make it work with the weight of two of us and the gear. He and Barry guessed it would . . . unless the snow was too deep.

The trip with Barry had been just perfect. Great trail, clear skies, plenty of dog teams to photograph. We had had a great time and I got some new images.

▲ The prop on Sam's Super Cub grabs the snow as it comes to a stop and sinks into the powdery snow.

Like clockwork, a few hours later, Sam circled over us as I stood by the trail waiting on a team that was just minutes away. The sun was going behind the mountains fairly soon, so this was good timing. Barry used my air-to-ground radio to talk with Sam and coordinate a landing area that Sam felt comfortable with. We just happened to be right near it. I shot the last team going by, Ramey Smyth.

I turned my attention to Sam's landing as I wanted to be in position to photograph him landing here as a memento. So I was all set and shooting when the plane sunk and I caught the plume of snow flying up.

When Barry and I arrived at the plane, we saw that it was a lot more stuck than it looked from afar. With not a lot of daylight to waste, we got busy. I tromped snow down with my feet and uncovered the skis using a grain shovel of Barry's. Knowing he would need a harder surface to take off, Sam instructed Barry to use his snowmachine to run up and back on the tracks Sam had made when he landed. Barry went to work widening the tracks and compacting the snow. With the wind calm, Sam planned to take off the opposite direction that he landed.

While Barry and I had our work orders, Sam dug into his trove of gear and got out a couple ropes. He tied a short one to the strut and a longer one to the tail. Barry used the snowmachine to bring the tail around some as Sam and I rocked the wings back and forth so that the skis would not bind as the plane was turning.

Sam asked Barry to hold onto the inside strut as I held the rope tied to the same strut. Sam got in, fired up the plane and added power. Barry and I held on as best we could so the plane could pivot and make a much sharper turn. The plane handled fine and we let go as the plane turned and lined up with the new, wider tracks. Sam stopped the plane, which did not have a chance of sinking on the new, compacted runway. We said our goodbyes and loaded up my gear.

Seated in the back of the plane, I couldn't help but think about Sam's concern of having enough room to take off. The plane had just sunk into the deep snow with only Sam and a little gear; now it was both of us and all my gear. As we accelerated down the slope and became airborne, I felt the anxiety fade, and slowly my thoughts went to the next shot. We flew west through the pass and onward to Rohn. Barry hung around long enough to see us safely in the air, then fired up his snowmachine, ready to ride back home to the Rainy Pass Lodge.

▲ ▶ Barry Stanley rocks the wing to break loose the skis as Sam powers up the plane to turn it.

▶ Sam and I work together to get an aerial photo along the Tatina River near Rohn.

6

Staying Alive

More than once, I've been told, "Jeff, you are the hardest working person on the race." While there are plenty who work harder and longer than me, I believe I work hard because I like what I do, and the Iditarod is a "target-rich" environment for photographers. Nearly everywhere I look, there's a photo to be made. That, combined with the great low light in winter and the fact that the Iditarod never sleeps. It's hard to stop working.

But everyone has to rest and eat sometime. As an official volunteer, I typically don't fret that I'll have a place to lay my sleeping bag and pad, but I also don't take it for granted, especially in some of the smaller, temporary, tent-type checkpoints. I ask before I plan to stay the night. I've spent my share of nights attempting to sleep outdoors in the bitter cold where I had to, but I'm over that now. These days I tend to stick with known accommodations.

No matter where I stay along the trail, free accommodations for Iditarod volunteers are not as comfortable or quiet as paid places for the press or tourists. I'm usually sleeping in a room—a cramped or noisy community center or other city building—with many other people. And a lot of those places don't have running water or other amenities.

Because the race is constantly going, and people are moving around 24/7, I try to lay out my sleeping bag and pad as soon as I know I'll be staying overnight. I'll put my stuff in a quiet, out-of-the-way place, so I won't be stepped on—like under a table, in a corner, or a back closet. Staying for free is great, but I can find a better night's sleep, and better internet access, by paying a small fee to throw my bag on the

▲ I prefer to claim an out-of-the-way place to lay my head. My bedroom for the night in this checkpoint was a closet.

floor of the local school. The best experience is when I get an invitation to stay in the home of a friend. That's a real treat: quiet *and* a shower.

Rarely do I spend two nights in one place, so each day I'm packing and unpacking. Consequently, I take serious the mantra "Travel light, travel right." I bring along ten days' worth of my personal gear—sleeping bag and pad, spare clothes, plus extra cold-weather outerwear—all in one duffle bag that can be transformed into a backpack. (Usually, I wear the same outerwear through the whole race and just change socks and long-john tops and bottoms each day or every other day.) I pack my laptop, battery

chargers, and cables in a small daypack. And my cameras all travel in a third backpack. That's three bags in all. If I had to, I could walk for some distance carrying all three, but I wouldn't want to.

Because I'm constantly downloading and processing my photos and then uploading them to the web several times a day, I rarely take the time even for a shower during the race, and sometimes I go all day on just a couple granola bars that I grabbed that morning. Thankfully, the Iditarod Trail Committee provides food at the checkpoints, usually through a sponsor. At the major "hub" checkpoints, McGrath and Unalakleet, which serve as a base for pilots and other volunteers, there is actually a kitchen with volunteer cooks. That makes eating a much easier endeavor. Just show up and eat. At the smaller checkpoints, it's more of a catch-it-as-you-can. At those places I will make a PB&J or cold-cut-and-mustard sandwich or some other easy meal. Often it's just a handful of granola or dried fruit. And of course, there is always the powdered drink "Tang" on hand. Tang is special to many of us who've been involved with the race a long time because Joe Redington Sr. was sponsored by General Foods and the Tang brand, so almost always there was Tang on hand.

After about twelve days' straight of eating nothing but carbs and pre-cooked food, and sacking out on floors in my sleeping bag, it's a treat to get to Nome. There, I usually stay with longtime friends like Chuck and Peggy Fagerstrom, or Pat Hahn and Sue Greely, where the food is fresh and good. And, at last, I can sleep in comfort between sheets. Another Iditarod down.

TIPS FOR THE TRAIL TRAVELER

- ALWAYS take earplugs when planning to sleep in a room with others . . . or any place that is not your own bedroom.
- IF sleeping outside, put tomorrow's long underwear inside your bag to keep it warm. You'll be thankful the next morning.
- RUB elbows instead of shaking hands to stay germ-free.
- IF you wear boots with liners, take the liners out of your boots *every* night and put them up as high (warmest part of the room) in the room as you can. If you're sleeping outdoors, sleep with them. Either way, in the morning they will be dry and make for a more comfortable and warm day.
- ALWAYS know the way to the outhouse or bathroom before the lights go out.
- KEEP a clock with a light in it and your headlamp within easy reach while sleeping.
- WHEN arriving at a checkpoint for an overnight stay, put out your sleeping bag as

soon as possible to garner a good spot. When sleeping in a corner or under a table, one is less likely to get stepped on or kicked in the head.
- WHEN packing your gear, always put the essentials that you may need later that day (such as heavy mittens or parka) toward the top, where they can be easily and quickly retrieved.
- ALWAYS carry a spare set of gloves or mittens on your person, like in your coat pocket or photo vest.
- The WATER PRESSURE is very low in many villages. To avoid a toilet getting stopped up, always hold the handle down a good twenty seconds or more until all is flushed away.
- CARRY two hats, one stocking for the above-zero days and one made of fur for the below-zero days.
- DRESS in layers. TOP: lightweight long-johns, medium-weight long-johns, heavy fleece pullover, fleece-lined windbreaker jacket, Gore-Tex shell, heavyweight down parka with hood. BOTTOMS: lightweight long-johns,

heavyweight long-johns, wind-stopper fleece pants with pockets, insulated bib overalls.
- The WARMEST winter socks I've ever owned are brands called Ultimax and Thermax, available through Cabela's and elsewhere.
- INSTEAD of using your sleeping bag's nylon stuff sack for a pillow, cut an old cotton pillow case in half, sew on some Velcro to be able to close up the hole, and stuff that with your clothes at night. Much softer and the cotton will absorb drool a lot better.
- DON'T buy the cheapest clothing, especially clothing with zippers. You'll regret it at 30 below with the wind blowing and it doesn't work.
- NEVER sleep in a sleeping bag with all your clothes on, especially not your bunny boots.

Mayday, Mayday, Mayday. This is Piper Super Cub 7685Delta. We've crash landed on Golovin Bay, 5 miles from Golovin toward White Mountain. Pilot Chris McDonnell, passenger Jeff Schultz. We have injuries. We need snowmachines to come from Golovin to rescue us."

This is, verbatim, a message I can recite to this day, because I radioed those words over and over again on the afternoon and early evening of Sunday, March 9, 1992, using a handheld air-to-ground radio. I transmitted the message for what seemed like an eternity on both the emergency channel 121.5 and repeated on the Iditarod Air Force frequency 120.6. The radio was borrowed from my long-time pilot Sam Maxwell. He had loaned it in case I wanted to talk to pilots while on the ground photographing. Thank God for that loan.

▲ My son Ben was three years old when this photo was taken a few months before March 1992.

▲ Four days before the crash, I shot Chris posing by the Super Cub after landing on a lake between Cripple and Ruby.

Chris and I had taken off from the sea ice at Koyuk shortly after I finished photographing the leader and eventual winner of the 1992 Iditarod, Martin Buser. This was Chris's first time flying the race this far north. We had covered 65 miles on our way to the White Mountain checkpoint just 18 miles ahead. Low clouds over the mountains prompted Chris to take a safer route along the coastline, over the sea ice and then across Golovin Bay rather than follow the trail over the cloud-shrouded mountains. We had just turned the corner from the Bering Sea coast and were making a beeline toward Golovin when we spotted a couple seals on the ice pack. I remember talking about them—it was the only life form we'd seen since leaving Koyuk.

The forward visibility looked fine as the village of Golovin crept closer, but the ceiling was fairly low and we flew at about 150 feet. We could see only a few hundred feet up the sides of the mountains near us. Our course took us directly over Golovin, and we could see the dark outline of White Mountain, our destination, some 18 miles ahead. Instead of taking the chance of following the marked trail directly across the ice to White Mountain, Chris felt it was a safer bet to follow the shore of the bay, where we could see willows and a few fish camp shacks along the shoreline. After a few minutes, suddenly those willows and shacks were no longer there. Or were no longer visible. I don't know which.

I felt the left side of my body pressing against the side of the plane. I knew the feeling from earlier flights, when a pilot steered the plane in a sideways attitude to either lose altitude or fly into the wind. Pilots call it "crabbing." But I also knew we shouldn't be doing that right now. Instinctively I called out, "Hang onto it! Hang onto it!" into the intercom.

My next thoughts are vague in my memory. I recall looking at my seat belt and either hearing or

thinking, *We gotta get out of here.* And in the next moment, we were outside the airplane. Neither one of us can recall *how* we got out. To see the airplane after the crash, it would have taken a lot of effort and gyrations, the flexibility of a contortionist, to maneuver our bodies out of the wreckage. How we got out, I can only chalk up to God and his angels.

"Jeff, I'm so sorry," Chris was saying. "I'm so sorry."

"What . . . what happened . . . where are we?" I managed.

"You're Jeff Schultz," he answered. "I'm Chris McDonnell. We're on the Iditarod."

I replied in a daze: "Yeah, but what's going on, where are we?"

We repeated that circular conversation for several minutes until our wits came back to us and we were both on the same page. We were alive, lingering in a surreal landscape, looking at the blood strewn about the wreckage, still not registering that this was reality.

Chris could not walk, having one ankle dislocated and one sprained. His right wrist was broken and he was nearly scalped, bleeding profusely from a gash

that would later require seventy stitches and several staples. Although I was dazed and foggy, I was in the best physical shape with all my limbs intact. However, it felt like my face had been hit by a freight train.

The wind was increasing. To escape it, Chris crawled to the fuselage, which now lay flat on the ground, and leaned against one side. I knelt and ducked my head though the window into the wreckage to retrieve our gear. In several trips, I dragged out most everything I could: packs, sleeping bags, pads, a first-aid kit, catalytic heater. I wrapped an ACE bandage around Chris's head and then put my beaver hat over it as tightly as I could, hoping to stay the massive bleeding. Chris managed to get into his sleeping bag.

Next I found the yellow Emergency Locator Beacon (ELT). I made sure the switch was in the ON position, then retrieved my handheld air-to-ground radio. Chris told me the emergency channel frequency. I dialed that in and found a *Wheep, Wheep, Wheep* noise. It was my ELT signal coming back at me.

▼ This front view shows the bent propeller and the broken windshield.

So I turned off the ELT and began the chant, "Mayday, Mayday, Mayday, this is Piper Super Cub . . ."

I knew we were directly under the flight path for Alaska Airlines and that a flight to Nome would be passing very soon. I thought I'd hear from them right away. But I was mistakenly under the impression that all commercial airlines were required to monitor the emergency channel at all times. No one came back, so I switched the ELT back on and then called on 120.6. No one came back. Chris suggested I try the local frequency 122.9. No one. I waited a few minutes and then repeated it all again. Still no one. My heart sank. I rolled out my sleeping bag to stave off the cold and continued the routine of making an emergency transmission every few minutes: first turning off the ELT, making the Mayday call on the emergency channel and the two others, then flipping the ELT back on.

Snow was falling more, and it was starting to get dark. We both knew that we should not allow ourselves to fall asleep for fear we might not wake up. Chris and I talked about life and faith. We prayed for God to hear us, to provide a rescue. Every ten minutes or so, I got out of my sleeping bag to repeat the radio and ELT routine.

❖ ❖ ❖

Just after 7:00 p.m., Will Vacendak, a commercial pilot with Bering Air, was in White Mountain and waiting on the tarmac for a late passenger to Nome. Just then a phone call came in to the airline's village agent. It was FAA regional supervisor, Jim Miller, with a report that there was an ELT signal originating from the Golovin area. The SARSAT (search and rescue satellite) coordinates showed the location at just 12 miles from where Vacendak was parked. He dialed his radio to the emergency frequency, and verified a signal.

With the marginal weather and so many Iditarod planes flying, Vacendak and Miller agreed it should be checked out. Will put his passenger in the plane

▲ Although neither of us remembers how we got out of the Super Cub, we most likely escaped through the busted-out windshield.

▼ A side view of the Super Cub with evidence of blood on the wing.

and flew toward the coordinates. Meanwhile, the weather had continued to deteriorate. Will flew over the site, but because of the ground blizzard, he couldn't see the wreck. At that moment, I was once more beginning my radio routine. This time, it reached somebody.

"Is someone trying to contact me on the emergency channel?" he transmitted. "This is Will. What's the problem?"

Hearing his voice, my knees went weak. I clutched the radio tighter and quickly responded, fearful that I'd lose contact with him.

Will directed me to repeat our names, our plane's N-number, and the extent of our injuries.

"Okay, hold on a minute," he said. "I'll get back to you."

Fear clutched me. Where was our lifesaver going?

"You're not going away, are you?" I pleaded into the radio.

"No, I will not leave you until someone is there to rescue you."

Tears sprang into my eyes. *Hallelujah! Praise the Lord!*

"Thank you!" was all I could say.

Will asked if I could see him overhead, his strobe lights or anything. No, I answered. Could I hear his engine noise? Yes.

"I'm going to fly a grid pattern over these coordinates. You radio me when you can hear me the loudest. I'm going to do that three times, okay?"

I honestly couldn't really tell what was the loudest, but did the best I could.

❖ ❖ ❖

As Will Vancekak was flying the grid pattern, a rescue party was being formed in Golovin. Having confirmed the ELT signal was an emergency, the FAA had called the village for help with a rescue operation. Leading the mission were two of the most experienced people in that region, brothers M.O. and Donny Olson. M.O. was a pilot; Donny both a pilot and a doctor. They had grown up in that region and were visiting Golovin for their mother's 70th birthday. Maggie Olson's party guests included a traveling dentist, a schoolteacher, several pilots, and a couple Iditarod race veterinarians.

The first hint of potential trouble had come between 5:30 and 6:00 P.M., when a pilot called the Olson home and reported an ELT signal that he'd picked up nearby. They knew that an ELT signal didn't automatically mean a plane crash, but could be triggered accidentally or result from just a hard landing. Without any specifics and with a storm outside, there was no reason to do anything at that time. The group was sitting down to dinner about the time that Will was telling me that he wasn't going to leave us.

"I had only finished about half my plate when a call came over the air-traffic scanner that a plane was down about 5 miles out on the bay," Golovin teacher Jack Davis later recalled. "We soon found out the plane's two occupants were alive and radioing a circling plane that relayed the message to us."

Within minutes, a search-and-rescue operation was set in motion. The Olsons contacted several snowmachine owners in Golovin. Donny, the only physician in the village, gathered medical supplies from the village clinic that might be needed. M.O. retrieved his removable GPS—new technology for the time—from his plane, and entered the coordinates that Will had triangulated from his grid pattern with feedback from me. Theoretically, with the coordinates, they could drive their machines to within a few hundred feet of us.

At least six snowmachines, some with sleds towing other rescuers, went out looking for us in the dark and in a ground blizzard where it was impossible to see more than 50 or 100 feet ahead. At times, gaps in the storm opened up, and they could see stars through the clouds and the lights of Will's plane circling. And yet, even with the coordinates and the occasional view of Will's strobe lights, they searched for more than an hour and still couldn't find us.

Finally, the searchers shut off their snowmachines and someone called Will on an air-to-ground radio. They informed him that they were at the coordinate

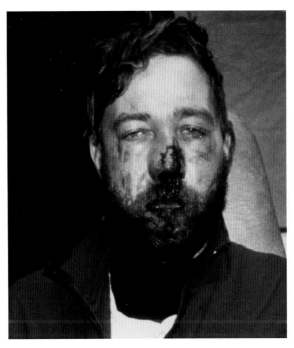

▲ I asked Mark Kelso to take my picture shortly after we arrived at the Golovin clinic.

▼ Recuperating in Intensive Care one day after the ten-hour surgery. My eyes were swollen shut, my teeth wired shut, nose packed shut, and tube in place.

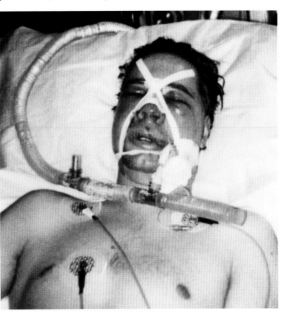

site, but there was no sign of us, and they could only see a very short distance in the blowing snow.

Will radioed the message to me. *Was there any way I could build a fire or had a very bright light I could shine?* We had Chris's catalytic heater, which he routinely used to keep the plane's engine warm at night. I had pulled it and a gallon of white gas out of the plane. Quickly, I simply doused the nine-inch wick with at least a quart of gas. For years I had carried my strike-anywhere matches in their waterproof container. I struck one match, and nothing. Struck it a few more times and still nothing. Tried match two, nothing, nothing. Three, nada. Time was ticking by. I turned to Chris.

"Do you have a lighter?" I asked.

Thankfully, he had a BIC lighter in his pocket. I didn't care that I had to tilt the lighter upside down to get to the wick. Even knowing that the flame might burn me, I was desperate to light it.

WHHOOOOMMPHHHH! A four-foot flame shot up and I quickly jumped back. Instantly I saw four headlights off in the distance.

As I later learned, Donny Olson was the first to get to us. Chris was still nestled in his sleeping bag, but showing early signs of hypothermia. Donny radioed to Will that he was with us. It was okay to leave. The others soon joined.

Donny would later say that he was hesitant to touch us, as he was not carrying malpractice insurance. But seeing how bad off we were, he knew he had to help.

❖ ❖ ❖

OUR RESCUERS WERE ASTOUNDED by what they saw of the plane. The landing gear was broken off, the propeller bent, the wings contorted—one forward, one backward—and the cockpit smashed. Richard Toymil described the scene later, saying, "The plane was all messed up. The windshield was broken, there was blood all over the dashboard, and there were bloody streaks where they crawled out."

Another member of the rescue party, Paul Claus, remembered, "It looked like a wreck that no one would have walked away from."

Chris and I were in good spirits when the team arrived, but, Claus, a seasoned mountaineer and well-known Bush pilot, was convinced that we would not have lasted another two or three hours given our injuries and the stormy weather.

It was Claus who helped me get onto a sled and into a sleeping bag for a ride behind a snowmachine. Before we left, I was coherent enough to ask him to get my cameras and film from my pack. No way was I going to leave them behind.

Five or more of the rescuers stayed behind to help with Chris as we pulled away, Jack Davis driving the snowmachine, and Paul standing on the back of the towed sled. Mark Kelso accompanied us for safety on a second snowmachine. We headed in the general direction of Golovin, but for nearly a half hour, we were bumping, zigging and zagging, even going in circles because of the storm. At least once Paul was thrown off the sled when they hit an unexpected snow drift. I had been rescued from the crash site, but another thought flashed through my mind: "Are we going to make it back?"

"We just couldn't get our bearings for the longest time," Kelso remembered. "I kept thinking, 'Poor Jeff. The crash didn't kill him, but this ride might.'" On one of the zags, the drivers crossed the Iditarod Trail and were relieved to see a reflective marker. With that cue, they were able to follow the trail to the village, straight to the clinic.

Meanwhile, Donny Olson was trying to get Chris warmed up before transporting him. He had put fresh, dry gloves on Chris and was rubbing his arms, legs, and chest. Wrapped in sleeping bags, Chris was then placed on a sled behind Richard Toymil's

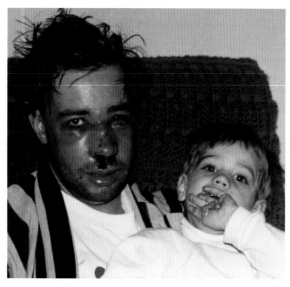

▲ About a week after leaving the hospital, Ben and I were photographed at home.

snowmachine and, accompanied by Donny, towed to Golovin. Four times on the half-hour trip back to the village, the party stopped so Donny could again rub his patient's hands and chest, trying to get his circulation moving. Donny said later, "Chris was in pretty bad shape."

At the clinic, village health aides Irene Aukongak and Sharon Henry were tending to us, besides Dr. Donny Olson and the traveling dentist, Dr. Mark Kelso. There, we were examined from head-to-toe and given warm IV fluids to bring up our body temperatures. Chris was wrapped in a thermal blanket. Warmer and more coherent, I asked if anyone had a camera and to please take a picture of me and send it to me in Anchorage. Mark Kelso obliged that request.

The medical professionals determined that, lacking a shoulder harness in the plane, I must have hit the pilot's seat face first and fractured my skull. Kelso, the dentist, recalled, "We cleaned out a lot of dried blood, but there wasn't much else we could do at that point. I could tell there was some fracturing

and his teeth had been pushed back and down. The damage was not irreversible." Nonetheless, Olson worried about my condition, thinking that there could be internal damage or even bleeding in the brain, given the look of my face.

A medivac from Nome had already been requested to fly the two of us to Anchorage. Such a flight presented some risks, given my head injuries, but my vital signs had stabilized by the time the flight arrived, and Donny Olson figured it was worth taking the risk.

As I was escorted out of the clinic to a waiting pickup to take us to the airport, I had to ask someone through my broken jaw, "Is it really okay to fly now?" They assured me it was. Chris was brought to the plane on a stretcher. Mike Owens, an EMT and nurse who I knew from Nome, was in the plane to attend to us. He and Donny Olson made sure that we did not fall asleep on the two and a half-hour flight to Anchorage.

This was becoming the longest day of my life and that flight felt like the longest ever. I SO very much wanted to just sleep.

❖ ❖ ❖

It was 4:30 a.m. when we were wheeled into the Anchorage hospital. I could see my best friend Ron Halsey, our pastor Richard Irwin, several people of the Iditarod Trail Committee, and my wife, Joan. She mouthed the words "I love you" as I passed by. I was touched to see so many people there at the hospital at that hour.

Little did I know that March 9 had already been a very long and difficult day for Joan. After several months of good health, our one-year-old daughter Hannah was running a 103.5°F temperature and began having seizures again. At 10:00 p.m., Joan had placed Hannah in a tub of tepid water to bring the fever down, and help control the seizures. About that time, she received the first of four phone calls from people involved with the crash. The first call from my usual pilot, Sam Maxwell, told Joan it was nothing serious, just some scrapes and bruises. However, by the fourth call, from Donny Olson, she knew it was serious as he told her of a bump on the head and potential broken jaw. All Joan could think about was a head injury and possibility of my having seizures. Shortly after midnight, Hannah's seizures started again, so Joan called 911 and paramedics transported her and Hannah to Providence Hospital. By 2:30 A.M., Hannah was checked and treated. She, along with our friends, stayed at the hospital and waited for me to arrive.

Chris's hospital stay lasted three days. He had surgery to repair his dislocated left ankle, fractured wrist, and nearly scalped head. And though I was much better off at the crash site, my injuries were a bit worse in the long run. There was too much swelling on my head to do surgery right away, so I had to wait days in the hospital until the surgeon felt I was ready for surgery. Cards and letters poured in from all over, and many visitors came to see me. I was even interviewed by a local TV station. I could not talk well, as I could move my jaw only slightly.

The first operation to fix the fractures was scheduled for four hours. Ten hours later, the doctor just said that I'd had enough, and it was best if he just stopped then. He had placed five titanium plates and twenty-four screws into the front and side of my skull.

When I awoke, my eyes were swollen shut, my nose was packed tight with gauze, my mouth was wired shut, and there was a tube down my throat. I couldn't speak. The only normal senses I had were touch and hearing. When a nurse attempted to vacuum phlegm from the tube, I freaked out and struggled against her, thinking she was trying to kill me. I was frightened of nearly everything. The only way I could communicate was by writing, but I couldn't see the paper I was writing on. My scrawl

▲ A month after surgery, Joan and I traveled to California.

▼ I stopped in Golovin during the Iditarod a year after the crash to thank as many of our rescuers and health aides as possible. I brought them a framed photo-collage as a tribute and thank-you gift. It still hangs in the clinic to this day. Front row from left is rescuer Donny Olson, his mother, Maggie, the late Sig Aukongak and health aide Irene Aukongak, and rescuer Mark Kelso. In the back row is me, health aide Sharon Henry, and rescuer Richard Toymil in sunglasses.

was often indecipherable to Joan, so that lack of communication made me freak out even more.

Three days after the surgery, I went home, still very much in a daze. For several weeks I just lay in bed or around the house, very selfishly expecting Joan to take care of all my needs. A month later, on a trip to California, Joan told me she needed to see a counselor, to get some help. That snapped me out of whatever funk I was in, and our relationship changed for the better.

On the trip to California, I looked like Frankenstein. People stared at me as we walked through the airport. Four more surgeries lay ahead, and I wore braces for eighteen months to realign my teeth. Today my nose looks like a boxer's after many bouts, but the only permanent issue is that my left eye waters a lot more than normal in a cold wind. A very minor issue, I might add.

Several months after the crash, rescue pilot Will Vacendak summed it up: "Those guys would have froze to death, except that a lot of things went right for them. There's the fact that I happened to be flying in the area, that I had the equipment to locate their position, that Jeff brought along a hand-held radio, that both M.O. [Olson] and I had GPS units, that there was a doctor in Golovin. If we hadn't been able to pinpoint their location like we did, we would not have found them until the next morning or when the weather cleared. That may have been too late."

I think the Golovin health aide, Irene Aukongak, may have expressed it best: "Everything seemed to be in line that night, everything fell into place . . . The Lord was with us, we were blessed."

NOTE: This account includes contributions from Alaskan author Bill Sherwonit. A few months after the crash, at my request, he interviewed the rescuers and others involved, and wrote an unpublished story.

7

Top Shots: f/8 and Be There

"What's your formula or secret to getting these great images? What camera and lenses do you use?" I often get these questions at seminars and such. I usually answer with a quote by the famous photographer Arthur Fellig, better known as "Weegee," who worked in the Lower East Side of New York City as a press photographer during the 1930s and '40s. He simply said: "f/8 and BE THERE."

That quote makes sense to me, because if I'm at the right place at the right time, know how to use the equipment I have with me, can find an interesting composition, and can predict or anticipate what may be happening in the next few moments, this makes all the difference.

In my twenties, I went to the Maine Photo Workshops in Camden, Maine, to take a few photo classes and have my portfolio reviewed. I asked a then-famous photojournalist for his secret to such great work. He told me straight up: "Jeff, I'm just faking it, like most photographers. Doing what I know how and experimenting when it doesn't work."

"Fake it 'til you make it," is how I took that. And now with digital photography, it's a lot easier and faster to experiment with what might work.

Bill Devine, the first official Iditarod artist, who designed the organization's logo, first introduced me to the saying "Even a blind squirrel finds an acorn once in a while," as he joked about some of my better photos. He may be right, but I'm also thankful for a God-given talent.

In the pages that follow are some of my personal favorites, as well as some of my most published images, and their backstories (whether it was prior planning, quick thinking, or a blessing from above).

When possible, I've included the setting and equipment I used—something for you folks who can't help but wonder.

WILLOW

Jump Start – March 8, 2009

When I saw these lead dogs leaping with joy and excitement, I quickly trotted to the front of the team and then purposely rolled, as gracefully as I could, from my knees to a prone position on my left side (while keeping my two cameras from diving into the snow).

The start chute was filled with nervous tension, created from the incessant, earsplitting barking of the geared-up dogs, the frenzied action of handlers jogging alongside the dogs, and loudspeakers blaring statistics of the on-deck musher.

Few dogs jump like this, so when I see one, I want to capture their enthusiasm and personality. But it's not easy getting into position for this angle among all the lunging dogs and handlers doing their best to brake them. Capturing the "decisive moment" is tough, too, because the jump is so brief, and the dogs often close their eyes. Or sometimes their bodies look contorted in mid-jump. Using a fast shutter speed and a camera that can shoot many frames per second is key.

This shot of Tom Thurston's lead dogs at the Willow restart in 2009 is one of my all-time favorites, mostly because of the happy look on the dogs' faces. To me, it looks like they're talking to each other, saying, "Woo-hoo! Let's-go-let's-go-let's-go!!"

Joy like this just has to make you smile.

Canon EOS-1D Mark III; 17-40mm lens @ 17mm; 1/1600; f/7.1; ISO 400

Canon EOS-1D Mark IV; 400mm lens; 1/800; f/6.3; ISO 400

Born to Run – March 7, 2010

Dog team!" came the shout from a volunteer trail guard. And sure enough, just seconds later, another team came careening down the hill from the Willow subdivision street level onto Long Lake. The last team had been by only two minutes earlier. I was still on my belly, waiting for the next one. I had positioned myself as close to the trail as I dared, not wanting to interfere with the teams. Attached to a tripod, my camera and 400mm lens was only about 8 inches off the ground, so I could get to the dogs' level.

A small crowd of fans and well-wishers stood on either side of the trail, waving and cheering on the mushers. The telephoto lens easily cropped them out of the frame. As this team came down the hill, I tried to keep the autofocus point on one of the lead dog's eyes. I cranked off some ten frames per second while panning the camera. Once they were too close for that camera, I quickly tightened the tripod head, grabbed my second camera with a wide angle lens, and attempted a second type of shot.

Back in the day, because the dogs run fairly fast and move like pistons, I'd have to pre-focus on a spot, shoot as many frames per second as the camera would allow, and hope that at least one would be in focus—and the dog's eyes would be open. It did work, but it was mighty slim pickings. With autofocus, it's almost like shooting fish in a barrel.

With teams leaving the Willow restart line at two-minute intervals, so many photo opportunities present themselves everywhere. I usually shoot about ten teams like this before I'm up and on a snowmachine with my assistant and driver, Ron Halsey, changing locations for an entirely new type of shot.

For Iditarod dogs, shots with this much expression happen mostly at the start, in the early parts of the race, when the dogs are well-rested, or when they're going up or down a hill. Otherwise, they trot along pretty nonchalantly. As with the "Jump Start" image, it pays to have a camera that can deliver many frames per second, because it takes only a split second for the dogs to look their best and worst. I was so impressed with this image because the dogs' tongues and heads seem like mirror images.

▲ ▶ In this attempt, I almost got all that I wanted . . . almost.

▶ A split second later, the dogs' eyes closed—it's certainly not the "decisive moment."

Canon EOS-1N; 17mm f/4 lens and Cokin graduated pink filter; estimated 1/250; f/5.6-8; Fuji 100 film

HAPPY RIVER

Bob Hickel, 1992

Hurry! Get rid of the snowmachine! Go down the trail and around the corner, and come back for me after the team passes."

In a panic, I was directing Barry Stanley, my snowmachine driver and friend. Very soon at least one team would be making its way to the bottom of the notorious Happy River Steps, and I'd found an incredible spot with the fresh snow, the mountains, a curved trail and a unique drop-off onto the river.

As always, I didn't know how much time I had to get into position and set up before a musher ran through the scene. I did a quick survey. I'd move up and use an extreme wide angle. While I prefer not to have unnatural tracks in the frame, snowmachine or human, I wasn't sure if there was time for a quick walk-about. I was also hesitant because the snow was unusually deep that year. I made the instant decision to be safe on both counts and just walk through the frame to the spot that seemed best.

As soon as I stepped off the trail, the bottom fell out, and I was up to my hips in snow.

Panicking, I picked my legs straight up, post-holing, and waded as fast as I could, picking my way to the highest spot, just 20 feet off the trail. All in one thought process, I switched lenses to a 17mm, my widest available, put on a split-colored pink filter, switched the motor drive to "continuous" / five frames per second, took an exposure meter reading with my handheld meter, and adjusted my shutter speed and aperture exposure to compensate for being in partial shade and the background in full sun.

Running dogs are eerily silent, and I've had a team sneak up on me many times. I listened hard and stared through the trees for any movement. It could be a few seconds . . . or an eternity. Suddenly, a pair of lead dogs came barreling out of the trees. I fired off fifteen or more frames as the team ran through the scene, and I got the shot I wanted.

▶ Finished shooting Hickel at the Happy River, Barry and our snowmachine are stuck on the uphill trail.

CAMERAS DON'T LIKE COLD

- **NEVER** take camera memory cards out of your camera on the porch of a school where they have metal grated stairs and an entry that allows snow to drop through the cracks.
- **WHEN** it's sub-sub-zero cold out, never bring your cameras indoors unless they are in a plastic bag. And even then, don't open the bag until the cameras have had a chance to warm up completely. Like the next day.
- **NEVER** breathe on your lens to clean it if it's sub-zero weather.
- **TAKE** a chamois with you to clean and absorb snow and ice off of lenses and eyepieces.
- **KEEP** spare batteries at the ready and always in a warm place on your body.

DeeDee Jonrowe, Eva Peak, 2000

Just go, go, go. Higher, higher!"

I was frantically motioning with one arm as I clung to the sled with the other. I was being towed with a snowmachine by Buckey Winkley, a big-game guide and true outdoorsman who lives at the Rainy Pass Lodge. It was the year 2000, and the late afternoon sun was illuminating the Alaska Range with alpenglow in a way I had never seen before.

Buckey and I had just passed DeeDee Jonrowe. From past years, I knew exactly where the trail headed. I looked far, far ahead and off to the left and saw a good-sized hill. I could visualize the shot I could get if we managed to get there and set up before Dee arrived. The pastel-lit mountains would be looming right behind her.

I asked Buckey to bomb down the trail, but to keep looking back for my signal to turn left. Then he should go as fast and high as he could, breaking trail up the hill. If we got high enough, I could get DeeDee and the team contrasted against the snow, rather than mixed in with the forest of spruce trees.

Once we stopped, I madly changed film to a full roll, marked it to process special (pushing the ISO from 100 to 400), added a split-neutral density filter (to compensate for my subject in the shade and the sun on the mountains), set up a tripod, and attached the camera to it. Less than a minute later, Dee's team filled the frame.

Immediately, I wished we'd gone higher, as the top of her head still overlapped the spruce forest background. But I still liked it, and so did the U.S. Postal Service. In 2009, this photo was chosen by the USPS to commemorate the fifty-year anniversary of Alaska's statehood.

▲ The U.S. Postal Service chose this image for a 2009 postage stamp commemorating Alaska's fifty years of statehood.

▲ I hold fast to a tow sled behind Buckey Winkley as he breaks trail to get around a musher.

Canon EOS 3; 70-200mm lens @ 200 and Tiffen split 2-stop neutral-density filter; estimated 1/500; f/5.6-8; Fuji 100 film pushed to 400

Martin Buser Storm, 2010

With Steve Perrins II as my snowmachine driver, we were approaching the summit of Rainy Pass and closing in on another musher. A light snow began to fall. We stayed well behind him as best we could to keep the engine noise from distracting the dogs. The long incline to the pass slowed the teams down considerably, and this section of trail was too narrow to pass without running right next to the dogs. Something I never do without the musher's permission.

Rainy Pass Lake was coming up soon and this would be our chance to get around him. Steve increased speed and got close behind. I was getting nervous as dusk was closing in—I had a plan and this wasn't it. We were supposed to be on the summit at least an hour ago to set up remote strobes for a night shot.

At first opportunity, Steve gunned the machine as we made a wide berth around the team, quickly getting to 20 mph on the flat lake ice. I hollered in Steve's ear, "Fast as you can to the top." I desperately wanted to set up at the summit and shoot this team. Being a mile away and with the even steeper terrain to slow the team down, I might just have a chance.

We bounced up the trail, as Steve did his best to go fast without tossing us off the machine, all the while I was looking around for "the spot." I noted that this year's trail across the summit did not take its normal course. The shot I envisioned wouldn't be there. Trail conditions, weather, and dogs—can't control them. I would have to adapt, quickly. We were near the top in no time and I directed Steve to park off the left side of the trail.

I went into "auto-photog mode." Creative adrenaline zipped through my body. I unlashed my camera pack from the back of the machine. The snow

▲ I grab a test photo of Steve Perrins II before he leaves me at the summit to start a fire in the cabin.

was caked on and required deliberate, hard brushing before the zippers could be opened. The light snow was increasing. Steve said he wanted to leave me to shoot while he went back to the Rainy Pass Lake hunting cabin, to start a fire. He'd be back in ninety minutes. I agreed and continued getting my strobe gear and tripod ready.

"Before you go, would you please drive down to the trail and let me take a couple test photos?" I asked. I only had one strobe ready—on my camera. The first shot was bad . . . way too bright. I fiddled for a few minutes, adjusting strobe output, shutter speeds, f-stops, ISO, shooting more test shots after each change was made. I was thankful again for digital photography; so much easier than film. Finally after about ten adjustments, I felt the exposure was dialed in correctly.

"Dog team!" Steve yelled.

"Go, go, go!" I yelled back. "See you in ninety!"

Steve was out of the frame as the team slowly came up and by me. I got off only two shots, because the strobe was using so much energy, it took the battery a full two seconds to recycle.

The LCD screen showed an okay image. Not exactly what I had in mind, but okay. Without knowing how long I had until the next team, I stayed near the

spot but decided to set up the remote strobe, figuring it would make the image look more three-dimensional by lighting up the rocks and snow in the background.

As I worked, I kept checking the trail for a team. I hooked up the strobe to the stand, battery to strobe, and strobe to remote receiver as the snow continued falling. Would the snow create a short circuit? I hoped not. A test confirmed that the remote was working.

I moved down the trail and placed the strobe, then returned to my designated spot. It was darker yet. I shot a test photo. Something was not right. I heard a light jingling sound, but saw nothing down the trail. It has to be a team, I thought. Caribou and Dall sheep around here won't wear anything metal. I shot another test. Dang. I'd planned this for months and now the remote strobe wasn't working.

Being a professional photographer, I did what we all do. Faked it. Made it work somehow. I again tested and quickly adjusted the on-camera strobe by pointing it nearly straight up to avoid an overexposed foreground and did my best to pre-focus on where the team would be. I didn't want to chance the auto-focus in this low light and perhaps miss the shot. Now I could hear dogs panting and spotted them a hundred yards off. As the team ran through the pre-determined and pre-focused area, I shot just one frame, then one more for good measure. This time the LCD screen showed the image looked even better. The lower ambient light combined with the strobe made the image pop that much better.

I shot several teams in this spot, as they were coming one, right after the other, but it wasn't until I got to Nome that I actually figured out who the musher was that was in the best of those images. Anxiety, error, hope, and a dose of "let's try this." At last, I had gotten the shot.

EOS-1D Mark III; 24-105mm @ 26mm; 1/2 second; f/4 with on-camera Canon 580 Flash pointed nearly straight up at +3 stops; ISO 800

Diana Dronenburg, 1989

I was doing my best to hang onto a dogsled, as I was towed behind Barry Stanley's snowmachine. My arms were aching and my feet hurt, but the sight of the mountains around me and the possibility of taking never-seen photos of Iditarod mushers in this area was a motivator.

A few weeks before the race, I had contacted Barry and Kirsten Stanley, then caretakers at the Rainy Pass Lodge, via their radio phone. Barry, who's also a hunting guide, happily agreed to take me by snowmachine the 30 miles from the Rainy Pass up and over the Alaska Range, through the 3,052-foot Rainy Pass itself, and over to the Rohn checkpoint. Kirsten had an old dogsled that Barry felt he could jury-rig for towing. We made it up and over the actual summit and passed one team on the way there. This was all new territory for me, and I was ecstatic.

Now, where shall we stop and wait for the musher? The trail narrowed dramatically. We could nearly touch each side of the canyon walls right on top of frozen Pass Creek. I spotted an excellent place above the trail, but it was inaccessible by snowmachine. We stopped around the corner, parked the snowmachine out of the way and began to trudge up the hill. Without snowshoes, we were at times up to our waist in snow; other times, we were walking on rocks. I was sweating, worrying that we might not make it in time to photograph the oncoming musher.

At last we reached the top and I found an excellent spot to set up. I was expecting the team at any moment. We waited. And waited. We chatted to pass the time, talking about Barry's big-game guiding and life at the lodge. Me, about why I would go to all

this trouble for a photo. And we waited some more. After an hour, we sat down, wondering what could have happened to Diana Dronenburg's team, which we were sure was coming. Suddenly the landscape moved, and my heart raced.

I stood and shot the team coming at us, big mountains all around—a brand-new type of shot for me. Diana and her team were directly below us, when she decided to stop. She put the snow hook in and walked up the line as the dogs sat on the trail. In moments, Diana had finished her team check, and they were on their way again.

▲ Barry and I wait near the summit of Rain Pass for a team to pass by. Note the snow shovel—an essential piece of our trail gear.

▶ In all the excitement, I fail to notice that Barry and I are casting a shadow in all the photos of Diana's approach.

One of the shots I took after that rest stop became one of my better-selling images of the Iditarod. It was also my first lesson in musher's time schedule. They can stop anywhere, anytime, for any reason. As I was editing the film, I learned another hard lesson: My shadow and Barry's were visible in all of the frames of Diana mushing toward us.

Canon F1; 35mm lens; estimated 1/250; f/8; Kodachrome 64 film

DALZELL GORGE

The Dalzell Walk of Three, 1993

The snow was crunching under my boots as I walked the trail on the floor of the famous Dalzell Gorge between Rainy Pass and Rohn, always a narrow stretch with a snow bridge and open running water. It made great video and photos, and even better stories of mushers crashing through the bridges and falling into the water.

It was a narrow trail and walking on it the same direction as the teams were heading, it was prudent to watch over my shoulder every few seconds so a team, silent as they are, didn't catch up to me. With my hat pulled over my ears and the snow crunching beneath me, it was possible that I couldn't hear the panting of a dog team behind me. I checked frequently. But sure enough, I failed to check often enough. Suddenly lead dogs were right between my legs and I jumped off to one side. The musher never saw it or me because the trail was winding so tightly. He passed by, and I had no chance to get a shot.

Just thirty minutes earlier, I'd been sweating heavily, walking backwards up a hill, bending and pulling on the snowmachine ski, as my snowmobile guide Barry Stanley inched the stuck machine up the long, icy hill. We'd gotten stuck because we were riding double on one machine, on a hill so icy that the track couldn't gain traction. I was sweating both because it was exhausting work, and I was extremely anxious. It was the last place I'd want to be if a dog team showed up.

This section of the trail had been cut into the side-hill and through thick trees many years ago. There was a steep drop-off to one side and a steep uphill on the other. There was simply no other way through this land than this trail, and if we were stuck

Canon EOS-1N; 28-70mm; estimate 1/250; f/5.6; Fuji 100 film pushed to 400

Canon EOS-1N; 28-70mm; estimated 1/500; f/4; Fuji 100 film pushed to 400

▲ Robin Jacobsen and his team seem confused about the trail location as it crisscrosses Dalzell Creek and winds in and out of the forest.

◄ Dan MacEachen maneuvers his sled on the glare ice to avoid the open water of Dalzell Creek.

► I was able to capture this image of Dewey Halverson at a decisive moment as he struggles with his sled before falling.

on it, a team would have to wait until we were unstuck to make it by us. Luckily, we made it to the top of the hill before a team came along.

We slowly made our way through the Dalzell, me walking a lot because I wanted to shoot pictures in various parts of it, maybe capture a crash in this dicey stretch. Still, while one musher might make a mistake and fall over or fall in or experience a catastrophe at a particular spot, that doesn't mean that any others will. So capturing a falling musher is really a luck thing.

In this case, the trail and teams afforded me wonderful opportunities to make distinctive images of just how difficult, unpredictable, and changing the trail can be within just a half-mile of trail.

Canon EOS-1N; 70-200mm; estimated 1/500; f/4; Fuji 100 film pushed to 400

Dalzell from the Air, 2005

I'm gonna need to make a quick left-hand turn soon lest we become part of the mountain." Pilot Danny Davidson's voice came to me through my headphones. "You see anything?"

"Not yet," I answered. "You keep us safe; I'll take the pictures."

We were flying over the Dalzell Gorge, and I was determined to take a photo straight down. I was hoping for an image of a musher and team snaking their way around open water and over ice bridges through this narrow section of trail. Danny rolled the plane hard left to avoid the mountain, and called over the radio to warn other pilots.

"Orbiting over the Dalzell at five hundred feet AGL [above ground level] taking pictures east to west," Danny said into the mic as we zigzagged down the trail, optimistic that we would "just happen" to find a team.

Typically I shoot aerials from the right side of the plane, out of an open window to avoid shooting through blurry Plexiglas, while Danny flies on the left side. We made pass after pass, crisscrossing the trail, each of us grabbing split-second looks at the trail. Finally, I spotted a team, but it was too late for Danny to get me into position. He had to make another quick, left-hand turn, lest the mountain thing happen. This time as he rolled the plane sharply to the left, I took that quick instant to shoot from behind his head, straight down through his Plexiglas window at the team below.

Thanks to autofocus and a quick motor-drive, I got a couple frames off. Only later did I find out that there were actually two mushers in the photo. This is one of those photos that demonstrates the age-old photographer motto "f/8 and Be There." Not much skill, but good instincts and a lot of luck.

Later that day, Danny's wife, Susan, saw the shot published on Iditarod.com. She sent me an email complimenting me on the photo, but she also delivered a scolding, based on the many flying hours she'd spent sitting next to Danny.

"I know what it took to get that shot. Stop doing that."

Canon EOS-1D Mark II; 70-200 mm @ 100mm; 1/1000; f/2.8; ISO 400

DALZELL GORGE

Canon EOS-1D Mark II; 70-200 mm lens @ 85mm; 1/8000; f/5; ISO 800

FAREWELL LAKE

Cracks 'n' Dogs, 2008

Danny Davidson's Cessna 180 was going as fast as it could into a serious headwind. He was managing about 90 mph; with no wind, we'd be doing 120 mph. As we passed over Farewell Lake, I could see that the wind had swept the ice free of snow. The deep green color was spectacular and pressure cracks made a wondrous spider web.

I knew this ice pattern could make a good shot, but would there be a team nearby?

On the far side of the lake, in a clearing, we easily spotted a team, but the shot was just okay. I wanted to wait for a musher out on the lake. The plan was to drop to 300 feet, put the musher nearly straight beneath me, and have Danny fly as slowly as he could. Danny suggested we approach the musher head-on, into the wind; otherwise, we'd blast by the team like a rocket.

The ride was bumpy, so I wanted the fastest shutter speed for a sharp photo. I cranked the ISO to 800 and shot at f/5, with a shutter speed of 1/8000th of a second, and put the motordrive on high for five frames per second. We made one pass while I leaned out the window and shot. I thought it was good, but I wanted another pass, just in case.

When I look at this photo, I am thankful for my experienced pilot. He's the one who timed a 90-mph airplane with an 8-mph dog team, calculating the wind resistance, and working the tail rudder, the yoke, and throttle . . . all this from the other side of the plane, where he couldn't even see the team. I credit Danny for making this shot happen.

Canon EOS-1N; 28-70 mm lens; estimated 1/500; f/8; Kodak Ektachrome 100 film

Witness versus Participant, 1990

Pilot Sam Maxwell was always happy to help me in my never-ending quest to capture images from unique parts of the trail, whether it was an area with beautiful scenery, a potentially treacherous aspect of trail, some odd terrain, or an area that I'd not photographed before. Sam was always game. Like most pilots, he loved a "mission."

The Farewell Burn, about 275 miles into the race between the Rohn and Nikolai checkpoints, was the site of Alaska's largest wildfire in 1978. It burned a million and a half acres. The trail through "the Burn" was often strewn with blown-down dead trees. For

◄ ◄ Directed by veteran musher Emmitt Peters, his dogs nimbly make the leaps and gyrations necessary to cross the nearly defunct ice bridge.

▼ Roy Monk pulls on his leader's harness to get his team started over the spruce-branch bridge. At one time the bridge had a snow trail on it. After many teams crossed, the snow broke away, exposing the open water below.

Canon EOS-1N; 70-200 mm lens; estimated 1/500; f/8; Kodak Ektachrome 100 film

Canon EOS-1N; 70-200 mm lens; estimated 1/1000; f/5.6; Kodak Ektachrome 100 film

many years, without much vegetation blocking the wind, the trail was free of snow, down to bare dirt.

Until a permanent bridge was built over Sullivan Creek in the late 1990s, the crossing was a challenge for mushers and trailbreakers. Instead of freezing solid like most creeks, the Sullivan almost always had open water gently flowing. Twenty feet wide and about a half-foot deep, it was a perennial hazard. Trailbreakers

▲ Sam flew, then positioned and timed the Super Cub just right for me to capture this image of a team crossing the trailbreaker snow bridge at Sullivan Creek. Deduction suggests that the musher led the team across and the sled just followed. After seeing this site, I asked Sam to find the nearest landing spot so I could to walk to it.

had to spend a half-day building a temporary bridge of logs and limbs for their snowmachines and the dog teams that would follow.

In 1990, we flew closer to the creek crossing and saw that this year was no exception. From the air, we could see open water and a partial bridge with a few teams approaching a few hundred yards away. Sam knew just what to do. He immediately slowed the plane with flaps and less power and opened the door and window on the right side as I instructed him on the angles I was looking for. We shot several teams from the air, then I asked if there was a safe place to land. Sam flew back over the trail looking for any place close enough to walk to the creek. He found a small swamp with black spruce sticking up here and there.

Having enough room to land is typically never the issue. Instead, the pilot asks: Will there be enough room to take off? Is the snow dry enough so it won't stick to the skis creating drag (therefore needing more length to take off)? How fast is the wind blowing and is it coming from the right direction to help us get off quicker? Are there any obstacles like trees hindering the potential airstrip? Are there any hidden obstructions under the snow that could potentially prevent a safe landing and take-off?

Everything was in our favor. Our landing was about a mile and a half from the creek. As usual, I was hoping there would be enough time for me to get to the creek and set up before another team came. Always a crap shoot, but potentially worth it. Here was another place and situation that I've never photographed, nor had I seen photos from anyone else over the years.

After the short landing, Sam put on the engine cover as I left with my gear. He said he'd see me later, or not, depending on how he felt about the walk. The trail was set up pretty well. I didn't sink in more than an inch or two as I walked and jogged as quickly as I could in my winter gear, cameras around my neck and shoulders. Exertion and the panic of a potentially missed shot combined to warm me up. Without missing a stride, I stripped off a layer to avoid sweating.

I got to the bridge ahead of any mushers and I quickly deduced that the best image would be from the other side, with the mushers coming toward me. Crossing the homemade bridge was dicey as I had to leap over the first few feet of truly open water, and land on some icy, uneven snow and ice-covered limbs. I made it with only one mukluk getting wet in the process.

Once there, it was easy enough to photograph the action. Of the two mushers who crossed while I was there, Emmitt Peters and Roy Monk, each accomplished the crossing with slight differences. Both teams' lead dogs came to a screeching halt at the open water. (After crossing, a wet dog automatically rolls in the snow, freezing any remaining water into ice that sloughs off.)

Emmitt, a veteran musher, who trained his team for years, simply commanded his dogs to go and, reluctantly, they did just that. The lead dogs jumped over the first section of open water and onto the snow bridge. A sign of a competent musher and a well-trained team.

Monk, on the other hand, had a leased team. He did not raise and train the dogs as pups and was more involved in training himself, rather than the dogs, during the few winter months before the race. The dogs were less likely to know and trust him. This forced him to walk up and guide them across the bridge. A tricky proposition considering there was no one to drive the sled and hold it back. Could have caused a pile up of dogs.

In situations like this, I weigh the benefit of dropping my cameras and helping, or continuing to chronicle the action. Guilt tugs at me, but I'm there to do a job . . . and so are they. I came away with some great photos, all adding to the story of what happens between checkpoints.

Canon EOS-1D Mark III; 24-105 mm lens @ 75 mm; 1/300; f/6.3 with fill flash; ISO 400

TAKOTNA

Happy Dog, 2009

Musher on the river!"

The spotter who'd alerted us was sitting near the window of the Takotna Community Center. Immediately, I joined others who were donning their winter gear and went out to see who was going to check in—we had about seven minutes.

It was a "normal" day in the 2009 Iditarod at one of my many favorite checkpoints, Takotna. I like it because it's small (I can walk everywhere easily), many mushers take their twenty-four-hour layover here (lots of photo opportunities), and I can stay in the school (good internet access and a shower). Plus, the people are as friendly as anywhere on the trail, and the food is great.

The incoming musher was Sonny Lindner. He'd already taken his twenty-four-hour layover at McGrath and was stopping only long enough to check in and out. The temperature was somewhere below zero, and the musher and team's breathing had created a light frost that settled on their faces. One dog in particular caught my attention. He had piercing eyes, frost on his face, and a fantastic, FUN, expression I'd never seen before. I zeroed in on him, got down on the ground at his level and gave my full attention to getting a good portrait. I used a fill-flash to get some sparkle in those captivating eyes.

The dog was anxious to keep going and kept looking around, anticipating Sonny's act of pulling the hook and leaving. He was hard to keep in focus. After getting what I thought was a decent shot, I ran to Sonny to ask for the dog's name.

"Symbol," he said. "But not the way you think you'd spell it. It's 'Simbol.' Not sure why, my kid named him." With that he pulled the hook and was gone.

Jennifer Freking and Gonzo, 2008

It was just before dawn and the morning sky was just beginning to glow—that time when the light in the sky helps dramatize a photo. I was in Takotna, where a glut of mushers were taking their mandatory twenty-four-hour layovers. There were plenty of teams and mushers to photograph.

I noticed Jennifer working her way up the team from sled to lead dog, as most mushers do, checking on the health of each animal.

I love capturing the loving interaction between the musher and their friends. I figured that when she got to her leaders, she'd be in a great position to shoot with that glowing horizon right behind her. I set up the tripod, knowing I wanted just a subtle flash to show the foreground, but still have her headlamp light the dog. As Jennifer moved up the line, I took a few test photos to dial in the just a hint of fill-flash. When she got to Gonzo, she checked his wrists for soreness and gently massaged them. I got off four shots of the tender moment before she was up and on her way.

Canon EOS-1D Mark II; 24-105 mm lens; 1/4 second; f/4 with Canon 580 flash straight up using bounce card at minus 2-second curtain sync; ISO 800

TAKOTNA

Canon F1; 17mm lens; estimated 1/250; f/8-11; Kodachrome 64 film

IDITAROD

The Bellies of the Beasts, 1989

Spectacular light, unusual angles, a "decisive moment," and great composition—those are important attributes that photographers strive for in an image.

In 1989, I was shooting my ninth Iditarod. I was yearning for a new angle, something I hadn't done or seen before. Above, below, side, straight on, I thought I'd done them all. But underneath, now that's something I hadn't tried. I'd recently acquired a new device whereby I could fire the camera remotely, with a cord attached to the motor drive. Time to try it out.

The Iditarod Trail trends mostly north-northwest, and the race is held in March, so most often, I'm shooting mushers with the sun at their backs. I wanted to be sure there was little room for error with harsh shadows. And because I was trying out a new toy, I didn't want an audience in case my test backfired. So I decided to set up outside the ghost town checkpoint of Iditarod. At this point, the trail is headed directly south, so the afternoon sun hits mushers and dogs right in the eyes.

I used my buck knife to cut through the snow's top crust and dug out an area for the camera with motor drive. I put on the widest angle lens I had, a 17mm. I pre-focused the lens for about 4 feet, set the exposure between f/8 and f/11 so I would get a lot of depth of field, set the motor drive to high (five frames per second), checked that the cable was firing the camera correctly, then put in a fresh thirty-six-exposure roll of film.

I carefully set the camera into the hole, low enough to not get in the way of the dogs, but high enough that the lens could see down the trail. I had to guesstimate an angle that might catch some of the trail and the dogs' feet, but pointed high enough to get their heads, too. Next I cut a straight line, just a few inches

▲ Shooting a test shot in 2011, some twenty-two years after my first under-trail experiment in nearly the same exact place. With digital cameras, it's much easier to know if the exposure and focus is accurate—or not—before the team arrives.

▲ A team approaches my buried-in-the-snow camera near Iditarod.

deep, to run the cable from the camera to the side of the trail. I laid one of my mittens over the top of the camera for protection and put a bit of snow on top of it for camouflage. I wanted the dogs to just trot over it without worry. I triggered one frame. It fired just fine. And then I waited, hoping a musher would show up soon, hoping the weather wouldn't change and ruin my exposure settings.

After about thirty minutes, I saw movement. A team was on the way! I clicked one more frame to set my mind at ease. In my mind, I launched my math skills: thirty-six exposures at five frames per second will only give me seven seconds' worth of images. And I've already used up a couple frames for testing. A team would be travelling somewhere around 6 mph. I figured I might have to stop shooting somewhere in mid-team to have enough film to get the musher and sled. At the least, I wanted one shot that I could already visualize: the lead dogs approaching the camera.

I crouched low off the side of the trail to be as inconspicuous as possible. But the team noticed me. Their ears perked up and some of them barked a couple times. As the lead dogs got close, I began firing the camera. In an instant, the noise from the camera startled the lead dogs and they jumped off the packed trail and into the snow. My heart sank. I stopped shooting.

Musher Guy Blankenship couldn't see what all the fuss was about. In just moments, his leaders had pushed through the snow, swinging wide around the camera, and were back on the trail. The team dogs seemed clueless, just marching over the camera as if nothing had happened, so I triggered the motor drive once again. Most dogs stared down as the camera whirred, but it did not stop them.

As Guy passed, he said, "What was that all about?"

"Camera in trail," I answered. "Is there someone behind you?"

"Yeah. Joe Garnie."

I was scared, realizing I could have caused a real tangle. Thankfully, these weren't the frontrunners, racing to win. Hurriedly I uncovered the camera, rewound the film, reloaded, and buried the camera again to photograph Garnie. Over the years, I would repeat the procedure with various results, but that first year, I learned a good lesson: "Don't fire the camera until the lead dog passes."

Northern Lights, 2005

Clear and cold. That's typically when the northern lights are most visible, although there's no way to predict them. I'm thankful when the lights come out earlier rather than at o'dark-thirty. "Jeff, you should have been out at two this morning. The lights were fantastic." I feel deflated when I hear that, like I blew it.

It was 20-some below zero in 2005, and I was in the ghost-town checkpoint of Iditarod, 55 miles from the nearest street lamp in Shageluk. The aurora was just starting to come out as a few mushers bedded down their dogs for a long rest.

I used a technique here called "painting with light," which is great for adding detail to the figures of dogs or buildings that lie in the dark foreground. Here, during a sixty-six-second exposure, I waved the beam of my headlamp across the dogs and sled in the foreground and on the building in the back. I was fortunate that musher Robert Sørlie walked through the frame for part of it, which created the light streak.

Kaltag 1989

◀ To get this scene properly exposed in the pre-digital era, I used the darkroom technique of "dodging and burning." With the shutter held open, I moved my hand around in front of the lens on the lower portion to block out some of the ambient light of Rich and Vi Burnham's house. That allowed the northern lights to burn in longer, making them more visible on the film. Because these were "by guess and by golly" exposures, I must have shot a half roll of film for this experiment, varying the exposure time with my hand moving in front of the lens.

Canon EOS-1D Mark II; 17-40mm lens @ 23mm; 66 seconds; f/4.5 painting light with headlamp; ISO 500; 2:31 A.M.

Canon F1; 100mm lens; estimated 1/500; f/4; Kodachrome 64 film

ANVIK

Barve in the Shadows, 1989

It's six o'clock. Clear outside. Time to get up."

I was sound asleep on the upstairs floor of the Anvik Community Center. It was 1989, and Sam Maxwell, my pilot, was waking me up. The night before I'd told him that if it was clear I wanted to be airborne before the sun was up, looking for a team on the Yukon where we could get some long shadows of the dogs and musher strewn across the snow. Sam, like most of my pilots, was all over the challenge. Doing something we had not done before. Airborne before sunrise, however, was out of the ordinary.

I jumped up and grabbed my camera gear. I'd leave my personal stuff behind, except for my sleeping bag—that was survival gear. I asked the checker on the way out, "Did any teams leave recently?" At least one had about an hour ago or so. Great news. We had a good chance of catching at least one team on the river.

It was clear and cold, below zero. Fortunately, the catalytic heater that Sam had put on the engine last night did its work, and the engine was warm when we got there. We scraped ice off the windows, took off the wing and engine covers, and climbed into the icebox Super Cub. The engine started up like a champ, and we waited for the oil to get to its operating temperature.

Sitting in subzero weather, not moving and not able to move, was not comfortable. I curled my fingers inside my gloves to warm them. I checked that there were fresh rolls of film in the cameras. Nothing worse than running out of film while doing aerial photos.

We could see the sun was getting closer to cresting the horizon. Sam taxied in the deep snow down the slough in front of town. The wind was negligible, so he took off straight in front of us. As we climbed up a few hundred feet, the sun engulfed the plane quickly, while the land was still in its pre-dawn purple.

Sure enough, within minutes we spied a team moving on the river. The sun was not quite upon it yet. We flew a few circles around the team, figured out it was Lavon Barve and lined up the shot I wanted. Everything was working out well. The sun would be rising perpendicular to the team—not always the case—and the snow around the team was clean and track-free.

As the sun crested, Sam lined up the plane with the sunny side of the trail and flew in a straight line. Sam opened the door/window and I shot many frames, bracketing the exposure so I would have at least one shot. This is my favorite of the lot.

Ed Iten in a Storm, 2003

I hunkered behind the snowmachine's windshield, traveling uphill and into fierce 25-mph winds near Cape Nome. Blowing snow obscured the ground below me, giving the impression that my snowmachine had lost contact and was hovering over the earth.

I had made an educated guess that I could make some good images in this treeless area of tundra that gives way to whiteout when the wind blows. This stretch of trail from Safety to the finish line at Nome is my last chance for trail photos.

The sun was in a slow descent, giving me lots of time to make pictures in low light. I had borrowed one of the trailbreaker snowmachines from Nome, and headed up the stark coastal trail to meet any teams I could find. Musher Ed Iten had left Safety and I figured I could get some shots of his team right around sunset.

The wind was blowing about 10 to 15 mph when I was 5 miles out of Nome. Still no musher in sight. My thoughts were in a tangle, as they usually are when I'm on my own in marginal weather: Do I dare risk going further for safety reasons? Is the musher really coming? Will the light cooperate? Should I wait here, go further, maybe have the opportunity to photograph him in several good spots? Or is all this just a waste of time and I really should just turn around and go back?

The further I got from Nome, the windier it got, the more apprehensive I felt. Now it was blowing 20 to 25 mph and the loose snow was swirling about 8 inches above the ground . . . just enough to obscure the trail. It was disorienting, surreal. Vertigo threatened.

There was no way to know where the trail was, except for the permanent tripod trail markers and the temporary lath that the trailbreakers had recently put in. I feared if I lost the trail markers, the tops of which are just above the ground storm, I could become stranded. I hadn't brought a GPS with me. So I followed the lath, from one to the next. I was dressed for it, at least, and the goggles/wind-mask I borrowed from my Nome friend, Pat Hahn, was keeping my face warm.

Then, suddenly, I saw what I was waiting for: Ed Iten was coming right at me. My adrenaline kicked up a notch. I whipped the machine around, motored to a spot I liked, took off my mitts and put on wind-stopper gloves to better handle the cameras, my brain burning through all the exposure settings I needed. I left the machine running, worried that it might not start again.

As Ed approached, I shot with a telephoto lens, then used a wide angle on my second camera as he went by. My hands quickly got cold. I kept the cameras around my neck, put my mitts back on, and raced past him to another spot. As I got closer, I noticed the backlit scene . . . the cotton-candy snow swirling around his team. I liked it. I motored closer then stopped hard, stood on the seat, and shot some more.

I hurried to pass him again, the wind now blowing sideways, and I found myself off the trail just enough to throw the machine a bit off balance. Suddenly, it was as if I were floating sideways. A weird sensation came over me. Vertigo. I resolved to hold my head steady, my gaze on the horizon, until my equilibrium settled, and it did, quickly.

Ed and I leap-frogged into Nome, with me stopping occasionally to shoot his team silhouetted against the sun setting into the frozen Bering Sea. And by the time I got to town, I was cold-soaked, chilled to the bone, but satisfied with what I'd captured on film.

Canon EOS-3; 35-70 mm; estimated 1/500; f/8; Fuji 100 film

CAPE NOME

Canon EOS-1D Mark II; 100-400mm @ 250mm; 1/2000; f/6.3; ISO 400

Karen Ramstead Fireball Sunset, 2009

I was really feeling the cold, having been driving a snowmachine for more than two hours. So cold, yet so determined to not waste the perfect sunset that I knew was about to happen. I was chasing musher Karen Ramstead and her team the last 10 miles into Nome, leap-frogging her and trying out various locations to get my pre-conceived shot of her team silhouetted against the sunset.

After failing at three attempts to get the shot I dreamed of, I finally found a sweet spot, parked the machine, and got down on my belly at a low spot in the trail, just as low as I could. From that angle, the sun was at just the right level and the dogs would be silhouetted against the sky. The cirrus clouds were moving in even more. I knew this might be my only take before the sun left. I waited and tried not to think about the temperature.

As Karen's team ran into the frame, I shot ten frames per second until she moved through the entire frame, then I panned with her for even more shots. The screen showed that I got what I was after.

As cold as I was, I couldn't help but follow alongside Karen and her team, a hundred yards or so off the trail, stopping a number of times to shoot all I could as the sun was lined up just right. I so wanted to get her with a tripod trail marker, too. When she was just a few miles from the finish line and the sun was completely down, I passed her for the last time and ran back to Nome where I photographed her crossing the finish line . . . a pretty standard image. I felt like I had earned my keep that night.

A day later, I asked Karen how she felt about me being out there both passing and following alongside her for so long. I didn't want to distract her and

Canon EOS-1D Mark II; 24-105mm @ 35mm; 1/1600; f/5.6; ISO 400

the dogs. She said it was no problem at all, she was glad I was out there capturing what she thought was a beautiful scene and thought I must be getting some phenomenal shots. Later, I sent her a large print of what I felt was the best image, to which she responded, "Just fantastic." And as it turned out,

▲ I shot this while leap-frogging Karen and her team at sunset—not nearly as dramatic as my final selection.

Iditarod's development director, Greg Bill, chose that image for framed thank-you prints to give Iditarod's fifty-five sponsors that year.

Canon EOS-1D Mark II; 70-200mm @ 200mm; 1/800; f/4; ISO 400

Picturing History

Lance Mackey, son of 1978 champion Dick Mackey and brother of 1983 champion Rick Mackey, was less than an hour away from winning his first Iditarod in 2007. And he was wearing bib No. 13, which both his father and brother were wearing when they won. And this was Lance's sixth try at the Iditarod, the same as his father and brother when each of them won. So, it was an Iditarod history moment for the books.

Usually, I'm not wild about covering the race finish. For me, the race is out on the trail, between the checkpoints, often by myself, or lingering in those smaller checkpoints, where the race is more intimate and exclusive.

When the first musher crosses the Nome finish line, the chute becomes a regular media circus, as many photographers and videographers are jockeying

▼ Overcome with emotion upon winning his first Iditarod, Lance gives his mother a tearful hug at the finish.

◄ The first woman to win, 1985 champion Libby Riddles, celebrates with her leaders, Axel and Dugan, and a bottle of champagne. In those early years, Iditarod had few niceties at the finish line. The dogs are sitting on a fifty-gallon drum.

to get "the" picture. I'd rather not even wade in, except that it is a necessary part of the story that I'm capturing. And, at times, it's an exceptional ending.

Like in 1985, when Libby Riddles, the first woman to win, crossed the line. She took a chance and went into a storm out of Shaktoolik, and that gamble gave her the edge to win.

I was there for the 1986 finish, when Susan Butcher began her four-win dynasty with her unlikely lead dog, Granite.

▲ The year 1996 marked the first of four wins for champion Susan Butcher. Here, she poses in the finish chute with her famous lead dog, Granite.

▶ Amid all of the noise and confusion of the finish chute, 1991 champion Rick Swenson looks at me to take his photo. He had walked miles in a storm to win the race.

In 1991, we all went to sleep in Nome expecting Butcher to win her fifth race the next day, then everything changed in a ground storm. It was Rick Swenson taking a chance this time, going through a storm to win his fifth race. The air was thick with emotion and excitement when he crossed the line. Minutes later, on the winner's stand with his lead dogs, Swenson asked "Where's Jeff Schultz?" I answered, and he looked at me to make his photo with his lead dog. He wanted to be sure I would get the shot for history. That was a proud night for me.

In 2002, history again was in the making as Swiss-born Martin Buser won the race waving a huge American flag in the finish chute. A few days later he swore an oath and became an American citizen, also in the finish chute.

In 2007, the year after Susan Butcher died, her husband Dave Monson and their daughters, Tekla and Chisana, ran teams on a portion of the trail to commemorate Butcher as the race's honorary musher. I was at the finish line to see them cross and to witness and record another exceptional moment, as Tekla, the spitting-image of her mom and dressed in her mom's red snowsuit, kissed her dad's cheek.

As Lance approached the 2007 finish line, the atmosphere was again charged with emotion. Many of us knew it would be a poignant time for Lance because, as he said, he always wanted his dad to be proud of him, and this was the moment. Lance would be the third Mackey to win, and he'd come back from cancer and addiction to do it. All that,

combined with his raw, honest personality, made for some great photos.

So I entered the media circus and was among the photographers bumping shoulders for the best position, capturing the images I set out to make. The interview process and photo session with his lead dogs went on and on. Still, I'm glad I was there to record it for history.

◄ ▼ A crowd circles the finish chute as Martin Buser, proud to wave the American flag the year after the 9/11 events, wins his fourth race in 2002.

▼ I love this touching moment under the burled arch as Tekla Monson, Susan Butcher's elder daughter, finishes her trek to Nome accompanied by her father, Dave Monson. She is wearing her mother's red snowsuit.

It had been thirty years since I photographed Joe Redington Sr. with Mount McKinley in the background. Since 1982, I'd always wanted to re-take an image of a team with a more compelling view of the Mountain. I found the view I wanted years earlier while flying low over the hills north of Talkeetna. The hard part was finding a dog team willing to make

DENALI

the effort at a crazy-early hour and do it at the spur of the moment when the weather would be just right. In the spring of 2012, it all lined up when recreational musher Jeff Hemann and his wife agreed to do it. This photo, a digital stitch panoramic, was shot on April 3 at 6:41 A.M. in Denali State Park. No mishaps and no blood this time.

KICK STARTER

Thank you, friends!

Kickstarter.com is an online fundraising website where creative projects are advertised to seek those who'd like to participate in funding them. In exchange, contributors receive various levels of rewards from the project. I am so grateful for the 321 people who helped get this book into print through KickStarter. You have made it the success it is.

SUPPORTERS AT $65–$90 LEVELS

Hayley Becker
Ray Bulson
Celeste Dela Calzada
J. Chairusmi
Bill Curtsinger
Theresa Daily
Ezra
Gary Gillette & Renee Hughes

Lois Greene
Coral Lee "Cory" Hilby, MD
Cindy Klettke & her Backpack
David Konno
Christine A Kuball
The Langberg Family
Ray & Fran Lockwood
Lynn McGlashan

Ann Pence
Steve, Noel, & Trevor Ramsey
Stephanie Ravensdale
Quinton Richter
Gary & Laura Samuelson
Marlys Sauer
Petra & Thomas Sbampato
David H. Shantz

Jim & Kathy Slouber
Susan A. Smith
Philip Thomas
Corinna Vigier
Matt Vodraska
Bonnie & Richard Wilsey
The Wood Caruth Family

LEAD DOG SUPPORTERS AT $125–$2,000 LEVELS

Art Aldrich
Denise R. Arthurs
Jim Ashton
Mike A. Aziz
Sivani Babu
Paul & Jenny Biederman
Bjorn, Magaidh an Ruadh & Stitch
Julianne & Bill Brackin
The Brautigam Family
Martin Buser & Kathy Chapoton
Glenn Cantor, DVM, Inge Eriks, DVM, & Emma Cantor
Randy & Carla Cheap
Tom Chesterman
Maureen Chrysler
Lynette Stinson Clark
Karyn Colman & Jari Nirhamo
Joel Cooke
Laura Crumley
Karen G. Czarnecki
Andy Davis
Ted & Joan Dederick
Christopher & Shannon deMelo
Jean M. Dieden, DVM
Stanley Diment, DVM
Martha Dobson
Doug Eckhoff
Martin and Robin Eckmann
Logan Engels
Fred & Carol Finke
Robert Finke
Alice Fitzgerald

Jim Flook
K. Flynn
Stan & Sally Foo
Laura Juliet Ford & beloved family
Joseph & Debraly Gamache
Wayne L. Giza
Dr. Harvey Goho
The Griffin Family - Tom, Carol, Anne, & Rebecca
Mark Hahn
Dan & Wendi Hale
Ronbo & Colleen Halsey
Kathryn Hansen & Steve Perret
Sharon Harker & Scott Bontempo
Isabella Heister
Kimberly Henneman, DVM, & Debbie Hadlock, VMD
John & Linda Higgins
Angie Kalea Ho
Vergil & Annemarie Holland
Jeannie Horvath
Kathy Hurlburt, MD/Forward Srvs.
Ronnie & Debbie Ingle
Michelle Jackson & Rodney Haun
Glen & Jan Jardon
Harry & Diane Johnson
Richard & Jo Purnell-Johnson
Edward & Patti Judd
Scott & Holly Kincaid
Jeff King
Bill & Cathi Kramer
Kevin Kramer

Susan R. Latorre
James Lebiedz & Robin Brandt
Pat Plunkett Likos
Kim Lintott
Christopher J. Mapes
Meredith Mapes
Chris & Aileen Marston
Sam Maxwell & Theresa Buzby
Bill Mayer & Karen Shoemaker
Kimberly McCreedy
Michael G. McNamara, MD, AKHES
Deborah Menendez
Jonathan Miller
The Morris Family
John & Arlene Murphy
Garry L. Myers
Karen Neff & Frank Evola
Janet Nelsen
Nick Neu
John R. Norris
Bruce S. Nwadike, DVM, MRCVS, DACVS
ONNIE
Alpha Lima Ostrowski
Dannie Pearson & Jackie Purcell
Greg & Patricia Peters
Linda & Dale Peterson
Stephanie Pilch
Jan, Kirsten, Heidi, & Erika Pleger
The Charles Preston Family
Ken & Kathy Privratsky
Leo & Erna Rasmussen

The Ratcliffe Family
Owen Mao Reid
Lois Rockcastle & Eric Noble, Alea Robinson & Andrew Noble
Scott Rosenbloom, VMD
Bill Sampson, DVM
Ron & Nancy Sanford
Carolyn A Saylor, DVM
Betty Schultz
The L.A. Schultz Family
Robert Schultz
Pam Schweitzer
Nate Shuttleworth & Valerie Baciak
Sirius Sled Dogs
Michael & Meg Smith
Patrick & Sharon Smith
Arin Smith
Jerry L. Spindler II
Barry & Kirsten Stanley
George Stroberg, DVM
JoAnn Sumrall
Antoinette Tadolini & Charles Clack
Alex P. Tatum
Nelson & Chelle Tromp
The Uhlir Siberians, past & present
Brad & Kelly VanMeter
Matt Vodraska
Bryan G. Wachter, MD
Tim Whitworth
Silas & Sofia Wong
Stan & Linda Young
Gary & Denise Zimmerman

KICKSTARTER KICKSTARTER KICKSTARTER KICKSTARTER KICKSTARTER